Dan McGrew, SAM McGEE AND OTHER GREAT SERVICE

Dan McGrew, SAM McGEE AND OTHER GREAT SERVICE

ILLUSTRATED BY MARK SUMMERS

WITH AN INTRODUCTION BY TAD TULEJA

A STONESONG PRESS BOOK

TAYLOR PUBLISHING COMPANY

Dallas, Texas

Illustrated by Mark Summers

Copyright Acknowledgments

We are grateful for permission to use poems from the following sources.

Rhymes of a Rolling Stone by Robert Service. Copyright © 1912 by Dodd, Mead and Company. Copyright renewed 1939 by Robert W. Service.

Rhymes of a Red Cross Man by Robert Service. Copyright © 1916 by Dodd, Mead and Company. Copyright renewed 1944 by Robert W. Service.

Rhymes of a Rebel by Robert Service. Copyright © 1952 by Dodd, Mead and Company, Inc. Copyright renewed 1980 by Germaine Service and Iris Davies.

Lyrics of a Low Brow by Robert Service. Copyright © 1951 by Dodd, Mead and Company, Inc. Copyright renewed 1979 by Germaine Service and Iris Davies.

Published by Taylor Publishing Co.
1550 West Mockingbird Lane, Dallas, Texas 75235

Distributed in Canada by McGraw-Hill Ryerson Limited.

Library of Congress Cataloging in Publication Data

Service, Robert W. (Robert William), 1874-1958.
Dan McGrew, Sam McGee, and other great Service.

"A Stonesong Press book."
Includes index.
I. Title.
PR9199.3.S45A6 1987 811'.52 86-30015
ISBN 0-87833-544-7

Printed in the United States of America

10 9 8 7 6 5 4 3 2 1

BOOK DESIGN BY LURELLE CHEVERIE

Contents

Witness To The Wild

AN APPRECIATION OF
ROBERT W. SERVICE

In the fall of 1893, the Swiss painter Karl Bodmer died at Barbizon. He was eighty-four, and he had lived in the French village for half a century, producing the forest views and peasant scenes for which the Barbizon School was well known. Most of this work was forgotten. Bodmer's enduring legacy is a body of sketches he made along the upper Missouri River when he was twenty-four years old. His renderings of Blackfeet and Mandan Indians, a small and uncharacteristic fragment of his life's work, are what we think of when we say "Bodmer."

Robert W. Service, another European visitor to the wilder shores of North America, suffered a similar destiny. In 1958, when *he* was eighty-four, he had been living in France and Monte Carlo for forty years. Throughout that time he had written verse almost daily; a checklist of Service first editions contains nineteen books of poetry alone. Yet his reputation rests on one volume, his inaugural *Songs of a Sourdough*, published when he was thirty-three. That book's most celebrated ballads established the author, forever, as "the chap who wrote McGrew and McGee."

This was not a fate Service deplored. Indeed, he encouraged the impression that the Yukon was his private claim. "The Shooting of Dan McGrew" and "The Cremation of Sam McGee," although representing only a fragment of his work, are certainly not uncharacteristic, and the poet himself, in 1949, gave this sound assessment of his fame:

> ...I fancy my grave-digger griping
> As he gives my last lodging a pat:
> "That guy wrote McGrew;
> 'Twas the best he could do" ...
> So I'll go to my maker with that.

It is entirely appropriate, therefore, that this new collection of Service poems should focus on the vintage Yukon period; throughout his own long Barbizon afternoon, he understood even better than his admirers that his destiny had been to sing of the wild.

According to Carl Klinck's biography *Robert Service* (Dodd, Mead, 1976), the poet was born Robert William Service to an English mother and Scottish father on January 16, 1874, in Lancashire. The family moved to Scotland when "Rubbert Wullie" was a child, and there he was farmed out to his paternal grandfather and two maiden aunts. Their household was pious, industrious, and dour, and the boy's impish nature surfaced early as a rebuke to what he called the Long Grey Town. In his 1945 autobiography *Ploughman of the Moon*, recollecting his "horror of the Scotch Sabbath," he confessed that his first poem was a mock grace that ended with the plea: "Bless the scones Aunt Jeannie makes/and save us all from belly aches."

High spirits aside, Service managed to absorb some pragmatic sense, and shortly after graduating from high school he was apprenticed in his father's profession, banking. For much of the following two decades, he was at the mercy of competing demons: banking remained his financial anchor, but his attention gravitated increasingly toward poetry and toward the open road.

The first round was won by the road; in 1896 the young teller closed up his cage and lit out for the Canadian wild. He landed in British Columbia with five dollars in his pocket, just as the Klondike was seized by gold fever. For the next seven years, as he proudly recalled later, he rubbed shoulders with various soldiers of fortune and "took a course in the College of Hard Knocks." It offered a varied curriculum. Between 1896 and 1904, as the mining towns boomed and then busted, Service wandered up and down the West Coast, picking oranges, digging railroad tunnels, running a store, teaching school, milking cows, cutting logs, singing songs, and playing to the hilt the self-styled role of hobo minstrel. In 1904, in Whitehorse, he took a job with a Canadian bank; for the following eight years, at Whitehorse and later at Dawson, he took on the part of good bourgeois, while entertaining his wanderlust by writing poetry.

Most of his verses saw only the inside of a bureau drawer. But the editor of the Whitehorse *Star* did accept a few for publication, and in the fall of 1906 he asked his contributor to write "something about our own bit of earth," to be recited at a church concert. Service produced "The Shooting of Dan McGrew." For obvious reasons, it never reached the church stage. But the budding poet's appetite had been whetted, and the next "bit of earth" he tackled came out as the ballad "Sam McGee." Over the next several months, during "lonely walks on the trails" around Whitehorse, he composed the rest of the *Sourdough* verses, and filed them, too, in a drawer.

They might have stayed there forever except that his landlady admired them and convinced Service to bind them into a book. Thinking that he could present such a volume "with apologetic wistfulness" to his friends, he retyped the lot, sent them to the Toronto publisher William Briggs, and tried to put them out of his mind. To his surprise, Briggs not only offered him a contract but claimed that McGee was the talk of the office and that they had taken 1,700 orders for the book on the strength of the galley proofs alone.

Perhaps it is a tribute to the early influence of his sensible aunts that, until he left the Yukon, Service kept his day job with the bank. The financial need to do so could not have been severe, for in the first year of its existence, *Songs of a Sourdough* went through fifteen Canadian printings. Royalty checks also arrived regularly from England (where the book saw twenty-three printings in three years) and from the United States, where it was published in 1907 as *The Spell of the Yukon*. Practically overnight, fame and fortune had descended.

Realizing he had struck a rich vein, Service wrote *Ballads of a Cheechako* (*cheechako* is Chinook for "newcomer"). Published in 1909, the book was, in Service's own words, a "self-conscious, premeditated volume." Written in Dawson, where the banker poet had been transferred by his employer, it played on the same themes—the allure of the frozen North and the infinite eccentricity of its inhabitants—that had made *Sourdough* a success. At the same time, with the gritty triad of "Blasphemous Bill," "One-Eyed Mike," and "Pious Pete" as its centerpiece, *Cheechako* demonstrated its author's growing mastery of his material. Service was right in assessing it as a better technical job than its forerunner and in claiming that it "expressed the spirit of the Yukon more than anything" he had done before.

The year 1910 saw a vaguely autobiographical and not very memorable Gold Rush novel, *The Trail of Ninety-Eight*. Two years later came *Rhymes of a Rolling Stone*, Service's poetic farewell to the North. A more disingenuous celebration of "robustness" than either of his previous books, *Rolling Stone* was also marred by a weakness for the O'Henry style trick ending ("Soldier of Fortune," "Death in the Arctic," "Barbwire Bill") and a penchant for doggerel philosophy ("The World's All Right," "Dreams are Best"). The grit and gumption in this volume sounded forced, as if Service knew his vagabond days were numbered and as if he was using a language half-forgotten. His apostrophe in "Good Bye, Little Cabin" is a fitting conclusion to the book. "How cold, still and lonely, how weary you seem!/A last wistful look and I'll go." He did go, in the summer of 1912, and it was the last he would see of the North.

Throughout Service's Yukon poems, one feels the press of three themes. The first is a raw barroom machismo—a celebration of those red-blooded Real Men who, when put to the test, will survive. Armchair Darwinism has always vindicated and prodded male vanity, but never more blatantly than at the turn of the last century. With Teddy Roosevelt in the White House, with Baden-Powell building "character" in the Boy Scouts, and with Kipling the most adored of English poets, it was perhaps predictable that Service's "Law of the Yukon"—an icy version of the Law of the Jungle—should have found an appreciative audience. "Send me men girt for the combat," he wrote, "men who are grit to the core." It was a typically Nietzschean demand, fit for the age of gunboat diplomacy, polar treks, and bare-knuckle boxing.

A corollary to this elevation of the Real Man is the literary man's adulation of "the folk." Bankers do not populate Service's poems. The heroes are fantasy foils: the staunchly working-class go-getters who can take a poke in the eye without flinching—and who keep their own pokes in their boots. Of the two farmhands recalled in *Ploughman of the Moon*, Service remarks: "They have never heard of Marcus Aurelius, but they can milk two cows to my one." That same bias for down-to-earth skills over "intellect" animates much of his work.

A second theme is that of the wanderer—another middle-class fantasy, but one which, in Service's case, he had actually lived. Service's protagonists do not have dreams of picket fences. They are the eternally dissatisfied, the dreamers—the rolling stones and "Restless Ones," the "Men That Don't Fit In." The theme of rootlessness, of course, had figured in North American culture since the days of Daniel Boone. In Service's hands, it acquired an honorific patina, as if being forever on the move signified not just an inability, or unwillingness, to fit in, but obedience to a vague, holy mission. Nothing shows banker Service's essentially romantic nature—or his internal sense of division—more clearly than his attraction to the Cain-marked isolato.

A third theme—the most encompassing of the three—is that of Nature itself: that untamed and untamable wilderness to which Real Men are inevitably drawn and where they are found worthy or wanting. If Service's affection for the rootless, indomitable male seems a garden-variety modern fantasy, the same cannot really be said of his reverence for the Canadian wild. If ever this bard of the backlands rises to the eloquence of his themes, it is in his evocations of what he called, variously, the Great Cold, the Long Night, the Great Alone, and the eternally brooding Great White Silence; the Silence, he says in "Dan McGrew," "you most could *hear.*"

The Silence has its threatening as well as its soothing aspects, and Service shows the threat with some subtlety. If the current generation of Real Men, fed on Rambo-unctuous pipe dreams, were to put together an epic of the North, it would be filled with ravaging wolves, skydiving claim-jumpers, and exploding glaciers. No such cheap thrills from Robert Service. You get the occasional raging river, yes, but for the most part the dangers of his Long Night are the insidious, nonexploding kind. They are the temperatures that stand at sixty-nine below; the six months without sight of the sun; and a flat stretching vastness so immense that it both intensifies and ridicules our mortality. The dangers of today's heroes are supremely physical. The dangers of Service's imagined Yukon seem almost metaphysical by contrast. They are the terrible beauty of recognition, the lurch into lunacy that can happen when we see ourselves mirrored in empty sky.

"The North has got him," Service says of Pious Pete, and it is by no means incidental that the typical Service hero is a little cracked. From the hooch-crazed stranger of "Dan McGrew" to the would-be suicide of "Death in the Arctic," from the eccentric undertakers of Sam McGee and Blasphemous Bill to the electrophobic Pious Pete himself, the real risk of the Arctic is not gold fever. It is the very extremity of the place—an extremity that may lead you easily from rapture to rupture, so that you begin to see, as a lost alcoholic may see and as Blasphemous Bill's friend does see, "the ice-worms wriggle their purple heads through the crust of the pale blue snow." In Rory Bory Land, as Service wittily called the Far North, the chances are always very good that the real and the fantastic may fuse.

This peculiar sense of the wild—the sense that its very beauty can be terrible—sets Service apart from the English tradition of nature worship and makes him very much a North American poet. In *Ploughman* he cites Henry Thoreau as one of his chief early influences, and it is not a surprising admission. Not only did Thoreau, like Service, play up the "recluse" persona to dramatic effect; he also anticipated Service's deep sense of awe for nature's power, and for the tantalizing terror of being alone. Service's idea of the Great Alone was, like

Thoreau's, quite distinct from Wordsworth's conviction that "Nature never did betray the heart that loved her." It is this more sophisticated, and very American, sense of wilderness that makes his Yukon scenes alluring, even today.

When he left Canada in 1912, Service briefly covered the Balkans War for a Toronto newspaper and then went to the antithesis of the wild, Paris. There he married Germaine Bourgoin, with whom he lived until he died. But there, too, the ice-worms intruded, in the form of the First World War. Service became an ambulance driver and stretcher bearer, collecting material for his fourth book of poems, the often touching *Rhymes of a Red Cross Man*. Published in 1916, it was received enthusiastically, especially in America. Carl Klinck characterizes it intelligently as displaying "little jingoism, but much disillusionment, and much compassion"—exactly what might have been expected from a man whose brother had been killed in action (the book is dedicated to his memory).

Rhymes of a Red Cross Man brought the chest-thumping period of Service's career to a somewhat jaundiced close. In its celebration of manly fortitude, its consciousness of the imminence of death, and its affection for oddball characters, the book shared themes with the poet's earlier work. Yet the exuberance of those themes was now muted, and the Kiplingesque hardiness was undercut by a sense of ambivalence and futility. If death north of Dawson came clean and silent, death at Verdun savaged the ears with the screaming of overhead shells and the rattle of machine guns and the moans of shattered teenagers dying. In the unnatural world of the trenches, "survival of the fittest" became a joke, and there was in the poetry of the stretcher bearer something more than the proudness of a drum. There was an awareness of the brutal and the stupid which seemed to question even as it applauded. It was as if the poet, thousands of miles from the Klondike, were beginning to see hung on barbed-wire all of those strong-willed men "grit to the core."

He stayed in France after the war, and for fifty years made Europe his home. He did make forays abroad. In the 1920s he visited Hollywood, where four of his works were set to film. In the 1942 Gold Rush melodrama *The Spoilers*, starring John Wayne and Marlene Dietrich, he made a cameo appearance as "the Poet"—scribbling "Dan McGrew" in a bar. And he did return briefly to Canada, although he got no closer to his old haunts than Vancouver. For the bulk of his life he tended his garden—turning out novels, an autobiography, a vegetarian manifesto called *Why Not Grow Young?*, and verse collections with chummy names like *Songs of a Sun-Lover* and *Carols of an Old Codger*. Comfortably retired from the open road, he quipped without bitterness in 1949, "Though I've one foot in the grave, the other's in the gravy." He had become the quintessential Bodmer in Barbizon.

And then his mind returned to the wild. Two months before his death, he sent *Newsweek* a poem about Alaska. He called it "Sourdough Star," in reference to the forty-ninth star that would soon be added to the American flag. "And now you call me," he wrote, "O how glad I be/to join at last that jewelled galaxy." Pretty awful stuff, but appropriate. You think of the dying Thoreau, muttering "Moose" from his deathbed and then "Indians." Or Service's own "Atavist," Tom Thorne, who, seeking Peace, understands "that the Lord has hidden it in the secret heart of the Wild." So it was with Service. In the end, as roses grew in the garden, this lover of the Silence turned back to what had always been his heart's deepest strain.

A word should be said of Service's style and of the fame he achieved in spite of it. I say "in spite of" as a sop to the Poetry-as-High-Art crowd, who have always condemned his work as mere "verse." Give them their due. At his worst (the Alaska poem is an example), Service was very bad indeed—much worse than Thoreau on his dog days and nearly as bad as Wordsworth in his dotage. But to his credit, Service was the first to admit it. Nobody knew better than he did that facileness could be a deadly blessing. In *Ploughman* he acknowledged this plainly: "Rhyming has my ruin been. With less deftness I might have produced real poetry." He called himself, unabashedly, a "verseman"; it was a sound, humble assessment. More precisely, we might call him a "coupletman": virtually all of his poems are end-stopped; the vast majority are rhymed *aabb* or *abab*; and his meters are invariably clunkety-clunk—you can march to most of them with no trouble.

But the style fit his themes and his talents. He was delighted when the Irish writer James Stephens praised his work as "very good newspaper verse," and unselfconscious enough to admit, when asked why he had never visited his neighbor Somerset Maugham in Europe, "I'm scared of those big fellows." There is defensiveness and resentment in the poem "The Man Who Knew," but for the most part Service seemed content to be merely a household name. And unless you are facile yourself, there is little point in criticizing Bob Dylan for not being Shakespeare or Bach.

Furthermore, when devourers of poetry call Service "bad," what they often seem to mean is that he is not *difficult* enough for refined tastes. Poets are almost as notorious as sommeliers and physicians for taking themselves too seriously. There are poets, as there are physicians, who honestly believe that "tremulous and diaphoretic" is a better phrase than "shaky and sweaty." Not Service. When his heroes get the shakes, that's what they call them. This is half the reason his verse is called "light." Light verse is verse that commits the unpardonable sin of being accessible to waitresses and mechanics.

Because of the elitism of poetasters in this century, poetry has become a cloistered art. Thanks largely to the influence of Eliot and Pound, it is now possible for preeners without either their diligence or their imagination to go around calling themselves poets on the strength of free verse and bits of Dante. They don't have to prove it in public, because the ancient tradition of recitation, which sustained bards from Homer to Robert Frost, has pretty much ground to a halt. As a result, the average guy in the street is about as likely to know a poem by heart today as he is to know Sanskrit or surgery.

This was not the case in Service's day. Even before *Sourdough* came out, he had made a reputation himself as a reciter of popular ballads like "Gunga Din" and "Casey at the Bat." That was no anomaly for the time. In the pre-electronic era, it was possible for roustabouts and ranch hands to know their Kipling as they knew the latest vaudeville skits, because poetry was still a public art. Service's millions of fans might not have been able to tell free verse from free love, but they damn well knew what rhymed with McGee. And they recited his rhymes—by the millions.

When I was a youngster in the 1950s, a family friend used to recite "Sam McGee." It would take him, I guess, about ten minutes—just the amount of time that your average kid today is able to sit still between commercials. In spite of the "obvious" rhymes and the thumping meter, listening to it did not seem a burden. We may have learned something from it, too: something about death, and far places, and human laughter, not to mention the pleasures of rhyme. I am not convinced that the age of Eliot and of television has done more to broadcast such lessons than pedestrian "Rubbert Wullie" once did.

The loss of such lessons is not trivial. The patent advantages of Service over the practitioners of High Poetic Art is precisely that he *is* accessible. You can still read "Sam McGee" aloud, and children will listen and delight in the images and the sounds. Maybe what they're getting is doggerel, but it's no more so than the album lyrics that serve as public poetry today. Maybe, in this age of private readings and public silence, poetic *cheechakos* need doggerel—just to whet the whistle. The priests of High Art may be right in suggesting that life is too short to drink cheap wine. But that argument only works if you've got a choice. If you need a fifty-dollar corkscrew to open the Margaux, most of us will settle for Mountain Red.

There is another, more "political" reason to be thankful for this reissue of Robert Service. Today, more than ever before, we need to be reminded of our limitations—of the necessary boundaries to human striving. For all his robust, "stout-hearted men" puffery, there is a current through Service's poems of enormous humor and humility—a current that is captured with great sympathy in Mark Summers's illustrations for this volume. At times when the Big Stick gets dusted off as an answer to international tensions, it is a good thing to be reminded of the lessons of a Red Cross man. And when bureaucrats threaten to surrender what is left of the wild to their cronies in blue suits and hard hats, there are worse poets we could turn to than Robert Service. It is Service's sense of his own human smallness, in the end, that makes him the right witness for the wild. Without that sense—without the common sense that says "I can take sixty-nine below . . . *maybe*," the Silence itself can be threatened—which is to say plugged in, amplified, and milked dry.

The faith of a new breed of prospectors says that the Silence, within and without, can be tamed—that, with enough mind power and horsepower and firepower, technology can solve any problem; positive thinking can make Our Way of Life universal; and every wasteland can be turned into money. It is not the least of Robert Service's lessons that, when you start down that high-minded, gold-drunk road, you end up seeing snakes in the snow, or watching clocks with a gun in your hand. When manly confidence becomes a national disease, look to Blasphemous Bill for a cure.

TAD TULEJA
Cold Springs, Massachusetts

The Rhyme Of The Restless Ones

We couldn't sit and study for the law;
  The stagnation of a bank we couldn't stand;
For our riot blood was surging, and we didn't need much urging
  To excitements and excesses that are banned.
So we took to wine and drink and other things,
  And the devil in us struggled to be free;
Till our friends rose up in wrath, and they pointed out the path,
  And they paid our debts and packed us o'er the sea.

Oh, they shook us off and shipped us o'er the foam,
To the larger lands that lure a man to roam;
  And we took the chance they gave
  Of a far and foreign grave,
And we bade good-by for evermore to home.

And some of us are climbing on the peak,
  And some of us are camping on the plain;
By pine and palm you'll find us, with never claim to bind us,
  By track and trail you'll meet us once again.

We are fated serfs to freedom—sky and sea;
  We have failed where slummy cities overflow;
But the stranger ways of earth know our pride and know our
    worth,
  And we go into the dark as fighters go.

Yes, we go into the night as brave men go,
Though our faces they be often streaked with woe;
  Yet we're hard as cats to kill,

And our hearts are reckless still,
And we've danced with death a dozen times or so.

And you'll find us in Alaska after gold,
And you'll find us herding cattle in the South.
We like strong drink and fun, and, when the race is run,
We often die with curses in our mouth.
We are wild as colts unbroke, but never mean.
Of our sins we've shoulders broad to bear the blame;
But we'll never stay in town and we'll never settle down,
And we'll never have an object or an aim.

No, there's that in us that time can never tame;
And life will always seem a careless game;
And they'd better far forget—
Those who say they love us yet—
Forget, blot out with bitterness our name.

The Ballad Of The Northern Lights

One of the Down and Out—that's me. Stare at me well, ay, stare!
Stare and shrink—say! you wouldn't think that I was a millionaire.
Look at my face, it's crimped and gouged—one of them death-mask things;
Don't seem the sort of man, do I, as might be the pal of kings?
Slouching along in smelly rags, a bleary-eyed, no-good bum;
A knight of the hollow needle, pard, spewed from the sodden slum.
Look me all over from head to foot; how much would you think I was worth?
A dollar? a dime? a nickel? Why, *I'm the wealthiest man on earth.*

No, don't you think that I'm off my base. You'll sing a different tune
If only you'll let me spin my yarn. Come over to this saloon;
Wet my throat—it's as dry as chalk, and seeing as how it's you,
I'll tell the tale of a Northern trail, and so help me God, it's true.
I'll tell of the howling wilderness and the haggard Arctic heights,
Of a reckless vow that I made, and how *I staked the Northern Lights.*

Remember the year of the Big Stampede and the trail of Ninety-eight,
When the eyes of the world were turned to the North, and the hearts of men elate;

Hearts of the old dare-devil breed thrilled at the wondrous strike,
And to every man who could hold a pan came the message, "Up and hike."
Well, I was there with the best of them, and I knew I would not fail.
You wouldn't believe it to see me now; but wait till you've heard my tale.

You've read of the trail of Ninety-eight, but its woe no man may tell;
It was all of a piece and a whole yard wide, and the name of the brand was "Hell."
We heard the call and we staked our all; we were plungers playing blind,
And no man cared how his neighbor fared, and no man looked behind;
For a ruthless greed was born of need, and the weakling went to the wall,
And a curse might avail where a prayer would fail, and the gold lust crazed us all.

Bold were we, and they called us three the "Unholy Trinity";
There was Ole Olson, the Sailor Swede, and the Dago Kid and me.
We were the discards of the pack, the foreloopers of Unrest,
Reckless spirits of fierce revolt in the ferment of the West.
We were bound to win and we revelled in the hardships of the way.
We staked our ground and our hopes were crowned, and we hoisted out the pay.
We were rich in a day beyond our dreams, it was gold from the grass-roots down;
But we weren't used to such sudden wealth, and there was the siren town.
We were crude and careless frontiersmen, with much in us of the beast;
We could bear the famine worthily, but we lost our heads at the feast.

The town looked mighty bright to us, with a bunch of dust to
spend,
And nothing was half too good them days, and everyone was
our friend.
Wining meant more than mining then, and life was a dizzy
whirl,
Gambling and dropping chunks of gold down the neck of a
dance-hall girl;
Till we went clean mad, it seems to me, and we squandered our
last poke,
And we sold our claim, and we found ourselves one bitter morn-
ing—broke.

The Dago Kid he dreamed a dream of his mother's aunt who
died—
In the dawn-light dim she came to him, and she stood by his
bedside,
And she said: "Go forth to the highest North till a lonely trail
ye find;
Follow it far and trust your star, and fortune will be kind."
But I jeered at him, and then there came the Sailor Swede to
me,
And he said: "I dreamed of my sister's son, who croaked at the
age of three.
From the herded dead he sneaked and said: 'Seek you an Arctic
trail;
'Tis pale and grim by the Polar rim, but seek and ye shall not
fail.' "
And lo! that night I too did dream of my mother's sister's son,
And he said to me: "By the Arctic Sea there's a treasure to be
won.
Follow and follow a lone moose trail, till you come to a valley
grim,
On the slope of the lonely watershed that borders the Polar
brim."
Then I woke my pals, and soft we swore by the mystic Silver
Flail,
'Twas the hand of Fate, and to-morrow straight we would seek
the lone moose trail.

We watched the groaning ice wrench free, crash on with a hollow din;
Men of the wilderness were we, freed from the taint of sin.
The mighty river snatched us up and it bore us swift along,
The days were bright, and the morning light was sweet with jewelled song.
We poled and lined up nameless streams, portaged o'er hill and plain;
We burnt our boat to save the nails, and built our boat again;
We guessed and groped, North, ever North, with many a twist and turn;
We saw ablaze in the deathless days the splendid sunsets burn.
O'er soundless lakes where the grayling makes a rush at the clumsy fly;
By bluffs so steep that the hard-hit sheep falls sheer from out the sky;
By lilied pools where the bull moose cools and wallows in huge content;
By rocky lairs where the pig-eyed bears peered at our tiny tent.
Through the black canyon's angry foam we hurled to dreamy bars,
And round in a ring the dog-nosed peaks bayed to the mocking stars.
Spring and summer and autumn went; the sky had a tallow gleam,
Yet North and ever North we pressed to the land of our Golden Dream.

So we came at last to a tundra vast and dark and grim and lone;
And there was the little lone moose trail, and we knew it for our own.
By muskeg hollow and nigger-head it wandered endlessly;
Sorry of heart and sore of foot, weary men were we.
The short-lived sun had a leaden glare and the darkness came too soon,
And stationed there with a solemn stare was the pinched, anaemic moon.
Silence and silvern solitude till it made you dumbly shrink,
And you thought to hear with an outward ear the things you ought to think.

Oh, it was wild and weird and wan, and ever in camp o' nights
We would watch and watch the silver dance of the mystic Northern Lights.
And soft they danced from the Polar sky and swept in primrose haze;
And swift they pranced with their silver feet, and pierced with a blinding blaze.
They danced a cotillion in the sky; they were rose and silver shod;
It was not good for the eyes of man — 'twas a sight for the eyes of God.
It made us mad and strange and sad, and the gold whereof we dreamed
Was all forgot, and our only thought was of the lights that gleamed.

Oh, the tundra sponge it was golden brown, and some was a bright blood-red;
And the reindeer moss gleamed here and there like the tombstones of the dead.
And in and out and around about the little trail ran clear,
And we hated it with a deadly hate and we feared with a deadly fear.
And the skies of night were alive with light, with a throbbing, thrilling flame;
Amber and rose and violet, opal and gold it came.
It swept the sky like a giant scythe, it quivered back to a wedge;
Argently bright, it cleft the night with a wavy golden edge.
Pennants of silver waved and streamed, lazy banners unfurled;
Sudden splendors of sabres gleamed, lightning javelins were hurled.
There in our awe we crouched and saw with our wild, uplifted eyes
Charge and retire the hosts of fire in the battlefield of the skies.

But all things come to an end at last, and the muskeg melted away,
And frowning down to bar our path a muddle of mountains lay.
And a gorge sheered up in granite walls, and the moose trail crept betwixt;

'Twas as if the earth had gaped too far and her stony jaws were fixt.
Then the winter fell with a sudden swoop, and the heavy clouds sagged low,
And earth and sky were blotted out in a whirl of driving snow.

We were climbing up a glacier in the neck of a mountain pass,
When the Dago Kid slipped down and fell into a deep crevasse.
When we got him out one leg hung limp, and his brow was wreathed with pain,
And he says: " 'Tis badly broken, boys, and I'll never walk again.
It's death for all if ye linger here, and that's no curséd lie;
Go on, go on while the trail is good, and leave me down to die."
He raved and swore, but we tended him with our uncouth, clumsy care.
The camp-fire gleamed and he gazed and dreamed with a fixed and curious stare.
Then all at once he grabbed my gun and he put it to his head,
And he says: "I'll fix it for you, boys"—them are the words he said.

So we sewed him up in a canvas sack and we slung him to a tree;
And the stars like needles stabbed our eyes, and woeful men were we.
And on we went on our woeful way, wrapped in a daze of dream,
And the Northern Lights in the crystal nights came forth with a mystic gleam.
They danced and they danced the devil-dance over the naked snow;
And soft they rolled like a tide upshoaled with a ceaseless ebb and flow.
They rippled green with a wondrous sheen, they fluttered out like a fan;
They spread with a blaze of rose-pink rays never yet seen of man.
They writhed like a brood of angry snakes, hissing and sulphur pale;

Then swift they changed to a dragon vast, lashing a cloven tail.
It seemed to us, as we gazed aloft with an everlasting stare,
The sky was a pit of bale and dread, and a monster revelled there.

We climbed the rise of a hog-back range that was desolate and drear,
When the Sailor Swede had a crazy fit, and he got to talking queer.
He talked of his home in Oregon and the peach trees all in bloom,
And the fern head-high, and the topaz sky, and the forest's scented gloom.
He talked of the sins of his misspent life, and then he seemed to brood,
And I watched him there like a fox a hare, for I knew it was not good.
And sure enough in the dim dawn-light I missed him from the tent,
And a fresh trail broke through the crusted snow, and I knew not where it went.
But I followed it o'er the seamless waste, and I found him at shut of day,
Naked there as a new-born babe—so I left him where he lay.

Day after day was sinister, and I fought fierce-eyed despair,
And I clung to life, and I struggled on, I knew not why nor where.
I packed my grub in short relays, and I cowered down in my tent,
And the world around was purged of sound like a frozen continent.
Day after day was dark as death, but ever and ever at nights,
With a brilliancy that grew and grew, blazed up the Northern Lights.

They rolled around with a soundless sound like softly bruiséd silk;
They poured into the bowl of the sky with the gentle flow of milk.
In eager, pulsing violet their wheeling chariots came,
Or they poised above the Polar rim like a coronal of flame.

From depths of darkness fathomless their lancing rays were
hurled,
Like the all-combining search-lights of the navies of the world.
There on the roof-pole of the world as one bewitched I gazed,
And howled and grovelled like a beast as the awful splendors
blazed.
My eyes were seared, yet thralled I peered through the parka
hood nigh blind;
But I staggered on to the lights that shone, and never I looked
behind.

There is a mountain round and low that lies by the Polar rim,
And I climbed its height in a whirl of light, and I peered o'er its
jaggèd brim;
And there in a crater deep and vast, ungained, unguessed of men,
The mystery of the Arctic world was flashed into my ken.
For there these poor dim eyes of mine beheld the sight of
sights—
That hollow ring was the source and spring of the mystic
Northern Lights.
Then I staked that place from crown to base, and I hit the
homeward trail.
Ah, God! it was good, though my eyes were blurred, and I
crawled like a sickly snail.
In that vast white world where the silent sky communes with
the silent snow,
In hunger and cold and misery I wandered to and fro.
But the Lord took pity on my pain, and He led me to the sea,
And some ice-bound whalers heard my moan, and they fed and
sheltered me.
They fed the feeble scarecrow thing that stumbled out of the
wild
With the ravaged face of a mask of death and the wandering
wits of a child—
A craven, cowering bag of bones that once had been a man.
They tended me and they brought me back to the world, and
here I am.

Some say that the Northern Lights are the glare of the Arctic
ice and snow;
And some that it's electricity, and nobody seems to know.

But I'll tell you now—and if I lie, may my lips be stricken dumb—
It's a *mine*, a mine of the precious stuff that men call radium.
It's a million dollars a pound, they say, and there's tons and tons in sight.
You can see it gleam in a golden stream in the solitudes of night.
And it's mine, all mine—and say! if you have a hundred plunks to spare,
I'll let you have the chance of your life, I'll sell you a quarter share.
You turn it down? Well, I'll make it ten seeing as you are my friend.
Nothing doing? Say! don't be hard—have you got a dollar to lend?
Just a dollar to help me out, I know you'll treat me white;
I'll do as much for you some day . . . God bless you, sir; good-night.

Grin

If you're up against a bruiser and you're getting knocked about—
Grin.
If you're feeling pretty groggy, and you're licked beyond a doubt—
Grin.
Don't let him see you're funking, let him know with every clout,
Though your face is battered to a pulp, your blooming heart is stout;
Just stand upon your pins until the beggar knocks you out—
And grin.
This life's a bally battle, and the same advice holds true
Of grin.
If you're up against it badly, then it's only one on you,
So grin.
If the future's black as thunder, don't let people see you're blue;
Just cultivate a cast-iron smile of joy the whole day through;
If they call you "Little Sunshine," wish that *they'd* no troubles, too—
You may—grin.
Rise up in the morning with the will that, smooth or rough,
You'll grin.
Sink to sleep at midnight, and although you're feeling tough,
Yet grin.
There's nothing gained by whining, and you're not that kind of stuff;
You're a fighter from away back, and you *won't* take a rebuff;
Your trouble is that you don't know when you have had enough—
Don't give in.
If Fate should down you, just get up and take another cuff;
You may bank on it that there is no philosophy like bluff,
And grin.

The Little Old Log Cabin

When a man gits on his uppers in a hard-pan sort of town,
An' he ain't got nothin' comin' an' he can't afford ter eat,
An' he's in a fix for lodgin' an' he wanders up an' down,
An' you'd fancy he'd been boozin', he's so locoed 'bout the feet;
When he's feelin' sneakin' sorry an' his belt is hangin' slack,
An' his face is peaked an' gray-like an' his heart gits down an' whines,
Then he's apt ter git a-thinkin' an' a-wishin' he was back
In the little ol' log cabin in the shadder of the pines.

When he's on the blazin' desert an' his canteen's sprung a leak,
An' he's all alone an' crazy an' he's crawlin' like a snail,
An' his tongue's so black an' swollen that it hurts him fer to speak,
An' he gouges down fer water an' the raven's on his trail;

When he's done with care and cursin' an' he feels more like to cry,
An' he sees ol' Death a-grinnin' an' he thinks upon his crimes,
Then he's like ter hev' a vision, as he settles down ter die,
Of the little ol' log cabin an' the roses an' the vines.

Oh, the little ol' log cabin, it's a solemn shinin' mark,
When a feller gits ter sinnin' an' a-goin' ter the wall,
An' folks don't understand him an' he's gropin' in the dark,
An' he's sick of bein' cursed at an' he's longin' fer his call!
When the sun of life's a-sinkin' you can see it 'way above,
On the hill from out the shadder in a glory 'gin the sky,
An' your mother's voice is callin', an' her arms are stretched in love,
An' somehow you're glad you're goin', an' you ain't a-scared to die;
When you'll be like a kid again an' nestle to her breast,
An' never leave its shelter, an' forget, an' love, an' rest.

The Soldier Of Fortune

"Deny your God!" they ringed me with their spears;
Blood-crazed were they, and reeking from the strife;
Hell-hot their hate, and venom-fanged their sneers,
And one man spat on me and nursed a knife.
And there was I, sore wounded and alone,
I, the last living of my slaughtered band.
Oh sinister the sky, and cold as stone!
In one red laugh of horror reeled the land.
And dazed and desperate I faced their spears,
And like a flame out-leaped that naked knife,
And like a serpent stung their bitter jeers:
"Deny your God, and we will give you life."

Deny my God! Oh life was very sweet!
And it is hard in youth and hope to die;
And there my comrades dear lay at my feet,
And in that blear of blood soon must I lie.
And yet . . . I almost laughed—it seemed so odd,
For long and long had I not vainly tried
To reason out and body forth my God,
And prayed for light, and doubted—and *denied:*
Denied the Being I could not conceive,
Denied a life-to-be beyond the grave. . . .
And now they ask me, who do not believe,
Just to deny, to voice my doubt, to save
This life of mine that sings so in the sun,
The bloom of youth yet red upon my cheek,
My only life!—O fools! 'tis easy done,
I will deny . . . and yet I do not speak.

"Deny your God!" their spears are all agleam,
And I can see their eyes with blood-lust shine;
Their snarling voices shrill into a scream,
And, mad to slay, they quiver for the sign.
Deny my God, yes, I could do it well;
Yet if I did, what of my race, my name?
How they would spit on me, these dogs of hell!
Spurn me, and put on me the brand of shame.
A white man's honour! what of that, I say?
Shall these black curs cry "Coward" in my face?
They who would perish for their gods of clay—
Shall I defile my country and my race?
My country! what's my country to me now?
Soldier of Fortune, free and far I roam;
All men are brothers in my heart, I vow;
The wide and wondrous world is all my home.
My country! reverent of her splendid Dead,
Her heroes proud, her martyrs pierced with pain:
For me her puissant blood was vainly shed;
For me her drums of battle beat in vain,
And free I fare, half-heedless of her fate:
No faith, no flag I owe—then why not seek
This last loop-hole of life? Why hesitate?
I will deny . . . and yet I do not speak.

"Deny your God!" their spears are poised on high,
And tense and terrible they wait the word;
And dark and darker glooms the dreary sky,
And in that hush of horror no thing stirred.
Then, through the ringing terror and sheer hate
Leaped there a vision to me— Oh, how far!
A face, Her face . . . through all my stormy fate
A joy, a strength, a glory and a star.
Beneath the pines, where lonely camp-fires gleam,
In seas forlorn, amid the deserts drear,
How I had gladdened to that face of dream!
And never, never had it seemed so dear.
O silken hair that veils the sunny brow!
O eyes of grey, so tender and so true!
O lips of smiling sweetness! must I now
For ever and for ever go from you?

Ah, yes, I must . . . for if I do this thing,
How can I look into your face again?
Knowing you think me more than half a king,
I with my craven heart, my honour slain.

No! no! my mind's made up. I gaze above,
Into that sky insensate as a stone;
Not for my creed, my country, but my Love
Will I stand up and meet my death alone.
Then though it be to utter dark I sink,
The God that dwells in me is not denied;
"Best" triumphs over "Beast,"—and so I think
Humanity itself is glorified. . . .

"And now, my butchers, I embrace my fate.
"Come! let my heart's blood slake the thirsty sod.
"Curst be the life you offer! Glut your hate!
"Strike! Strike, you dogs! I'll *not* deny my God."

I saw the spears that seemed a-leap to slay,
All quiver earthward at the headman's nod;
And in a daze of dream I heard him say:
"Go, set him free who serves so well his God!"

The Ballad Of Blasphemous Bill

I took a contract to bury the body of blasphemous Bill MacKie,
Whenever, wherever or whatsoever the manner of death he die—
Whether he die in the light o' day or under the peak-faced moon;
In cabin or dance-hall, camp or dive, mucklucks or patent shoon;
On velvet tundra or virgin peak, by glacier, drift or draw;
In muskeg hollow or canyon gloom, by avalanche, fang or claw;
By battle, murder or sudden wealth, by pestilence, hooch or lead—
I swore on the Book I would follow and look till I found my tombless dead.

For Bill was a dainty kind of cuss, and his mind was mighty sot
On a dinky patch with flowers and grass in a civilized bone-yard lot.
And where he died or how he died, it didn't matter a damn
So long as he had a grave with frills and a tombstone "epigram."
So I promised him, and he paid the price in good cheechako coin
(Which the same I blowed in that very night down in the Tenderloin).
Then I painted a three-foot slab of pine: "Here lies poor Bill MacKie,"
And I hung it up on my cabin wall and I waited for Bill to die.

Years passed away, and at last one day came a squaw with a story strange,
Of a long-deserted line of traps 'way back of the Bighorn range;

Of a little hut by the great divide, and a white man stiff and still,
Lying there by his lonesome self, and I figured it must be Bill.
So I thought of the contract I'd made with him, and I took down
from the shelf
The swell black box with the silver plate he'd picked out for
hisself;
And I packed it full of grub and "hooch," and I slung it on the
sleigh;
Then I harnessed up my team of dogs and was off at dawn of day.

You know what it's like in the Yukon wild when it's sixty-nine
below;
When the ice-worms wriggle their purple heads through the
crust of the pale blue snow;
When the pine-trees crack like little guns in the silence of the
wood,
And the icicles hang down like tusks under the parka hood;
When the stove-pipe smoke breaks sudden off, and the sky is
weirdly lit,
And the careless feel of a bit of steel burns like a red-hot spit;
When the mercury is a frozen ball, and the frost-fiend stalks to
kill—
Well, it was just like that that day when I set out to look for Bill.

Oh, the awful hush that seemed to crush me down on every
hand,
As I blundered blind with a trail to find through that blank and
bitter land;
Half dazed, half crazed in the winter wild, with its grim heart-
breaking woes,
And the ruthless strife for a grip on life that only the sourdough
knows!
North by the compass, North I pressed; river and peak and plain
Passed like a dream I slept to lose and I waked to dream again.

River and plain and mighty peak—and who could stand un-
awed?
As their summits blazed, he could stand undazed at the foot of
the throne of God.

North, aye, North, through a land accurst, shunned by the scouring brutes,
And all I heard was my own harsh word and the whine of the malamutes,
Till at last I came to a cabin squat, built in the side of a hill,
And I burst in the door, and there on the floor, frozen to death, lay Bill.

Ice, white ice, like a winding-sheet, sheathing each smoke-grimed wall;
Ice on the stove-pipe, ice on the bed, ice gleaming over all;
Sparkling ice on the dead man's chest, glittering ice in his hair,
Ice on his fingers, ice in his heart, ice in his glassy stare;
Hard as a log and trussed like a frog, with his arms and legs outspread.
I gazed at the coffin I'd brought for him, and I gazed at the gruesome dead,
And at last I spoke: "Bill liked his joke; but still, goldarn his eyes,
A man had ought to consider his mates in the way he goes and dies."

Have you ever stood in an Arctic hut in the shadow of the Pole,
With a little coffin six by three and a grief you can't control?
Have you ever sat by a frozen corpse that looks at you with a grin,
And that seems to say: "You may try all day, but you'll never jam me in"?
I'm not a man of the quitting kind, but I never felt so blue
As I sat there gazing at that stiff and studying what I'd do.
Then I rose and I kicked off the husky dogs that were nosing round about,
And I lit a roaring fire in the stove, and I started to thaw Bill out.

Well, I thawed and thawed for thirteen days, but it didn't seem no good;
His arms and legs stuck out like pegs, as if they was made of wood.
Till at last I said: "It ain't no use—he's froze too hard to thaw;
He's obstinate, and he won't lie straight, so I guess I got to—*saw*."

So I sawed off poor Bill's arms and legs, and I laid him snug and straight
In the little coffin he picked hisself, with the dinky silver plate,
And I came nigh near to shedding a tear as I nailed him safely down;
Then I stowed him away in my Yukon sleigh, and I started back to town.

So I buried him as the contract was in a narrow grave and deep,
And there he's waiting the Great Clean-up, when the Judgment sluice-heads sweep;
And I smoke my pipe and I meditate in the light of the Midnight Sun,
And sometimes I wonder if they *was*, the awful things I done.
And as I sit and the parson talks, expounding of the Law,
I often think of poor old Bill—*and how hard he was to saw.*

The Black Sheep

"The aristocratic ne'er-do-well in Canada frequently finds his way into the ranks of the Royal North-West Mounted Police."—*Extract.*

Hark to the ewe that bore him:
"What has muddied the strain?
Never his brothers before him
Showed the hint of a stain."
Hark to the tups and wethers;
Hark to the old gray ram:
"We're all of us white, but he's black as night,
And he'll never be worth a damn."

I'm up on the bally wood-pile at the back of the barracks yard;
"A damned disgrace to the force, sir," with a comrade standing guard;
Making the bluff I'm busy, doing my six months hard.

"Six months hard and dismissed, sir." Isn't that rather hell?
And all because of the liquor laws and the wiles of a native belle—
Some "hooch" I gave to a siwash brave who swore that he wouldn't tell.

At least they *say* that I did it. It's so in the town report.
All that I can recall is a night of revel and sport,
When I woke with a "head" in the guard-room, and they dragged me sick into court.

And the O.C. said: "You are guilty," and I said never a word;
For, hang it, you see I couldn't—I didn't know *what* had occurred,
And, under the circumstances, denial would be absurd.

But the one that cooked my bacon was Grubbe, of the City
Patrol.
He fagged for my room at Eton, and didn't I devil his soul!
And now he is getting even, landing me down in the hole.

Plugging away on the wood-pile, doing chores round the square.
There goes an officer's lady—gives me a haughty stare—
Me that's an earl's own nephew—that is the hardest to bear.

To think of the poor old mater awaiting her prodigal son.
Tho' I broke her heart with my folly, I was always the white-
haired one.
(That fatted calf that they're cooking will surely be overdone.)

I'll go back and yarn to the Bishop; I'll dance with the village
belle;
I'll hand round tea to the ladies, and everything will be well.
Where I have been won't matter; what I have seen I won't tell.

I'll soar to their ken like a comet. They'll see me with never a
stain;
But will they reform me?—far from it. We pay for our pleasure
with pain;
But the dog will return to his vomit, the hog to his wallow again.

I've chewed on the rind of creation, and bitter I've tasted the
same;
Stacked up against hell and damnation, I've managed to stay in
the game;
I've had my moments of sorrow; I've had my seasons of shame.

That's past; when one's nature's a cracked one, it's too jolly hard
to mend.
So long as the road is level, so long as I've cash to spend,
I'm bound to go to the devil, and it's all the same in the end.

The bugle is sounding for stables; the men troop off through
the gloom;
An orderly laying the tables sings in the bright mess-room.
(I'll wash in the prison bucket, and brush with the prison
broom.)

I'll lie in my cell and listen; I'll wish that I couldn't hear
The laugh and the chaff of the fellows swigging the canteen
    beer;
The nasal tone of the gramophone playing "The Bandolier."

And it seems to me, though it's misty, that night of the flowing
    bowl,
That the man who potlatched the whiskey and landed me into
    the hole
*Was Grubbe, that unmerciful bounder, Grubbe, of the City
    Patrol.*

The Harpy

There was a woman, and she was wise; woefully wise was she;
She was old, so old, yet her years all told were but a score and three;
And she knew by heart, from finish to start, the Book of Iniquity.

There is no hope for such as I on earth, nor yet in Heaven;
Unloved I live, unloved I die, unpitied, unforgiven;
A loathèd jade, I ply my trade, unhallowed and unshriven.

I paint my cheeks, for they are white, and cheeks of chalk men hate;
Mine eyes with wine I make them shine, that man may seek and sate;
With overhead a lamp of red I sit me down and wait

Until they come, the nightly scum, with drunken eyes aflame;
Your sweethearts, sons, ye scornful ones—'tis I who know their shame.
The gods, ye see, are brutes to me—and so I play my game.

For life is not the thing we thought, and not the thing we plan;
And Woman in a bitter world must do the best she can—
Must yield the stroke, and bear the yoke, and serve the will of man;

Must serve his need and ever feed the flame of his desire,
Though be she loved for love alone, or be she loved for hire;
For every man since life began is tainted with the mire.

And though you know he love you so and set you on love's throne;

Yet let your eyes but mock his sighs, and let your heart be stone,
Lest you be left (as I was left) attainted and alone.

From love's close kiss to hell's abyss is one sheer flight, I trow,
And wedding ring and bridal bell are will-o'-wisps of woe,
And 'tis not wise to love too well, and this all women know.

Wherefore, the wolf-pack having gorged upon the lamb, their
prey,
With siren smile and serpent guile I make the wolf-pack pay—
With velvet paws and flensing claws, a tigress roused to slay.

One who in youth sought truest truth and found a devil's lies;
A symbol of the sin of man, a human sacrifice.
Yet shall I blame on man the shame? Could it be otherwise?

Was I not born to walk in scorn where others walk in pride?
The Maker marred, and, evil-starred, I drift upon His tide;
And He alone shall judge His own, so I His judgment bide.

Fate has written a tragedy; its name is "The Human Heart."
The Theatre is the House of Life, Woman the mummer's part;
The Devil enters the prompter's box and the play is ready to
start.

Over The Parapet

All day long when the shells sail over
I stand at the sandbags and take my chance;
But at night, at night I'm reckless rover,
And over the parapet gleams Romance.
Romance! Romance! How I've dreamed it, writing
Dreary old records of money and mart,
Me with my head chuckful of fighting
And the blood of vikings to thrill my heart.

But little I thought that my time was coming,
Sudden and splendid, supreme and soon;
And here I am with the bullets humming
As I crawl and I curse the light of the moon.
Out alone, for adventure thirsting,
Out in mysterious No Man's Land;
Prone with the dead when a star-shell, bursting,
Flares on the horrors on every hand.
There are ruby stars and they drip and wiggle;
And the grasses gleam in a light blood-red;
There are emerald stars, and their tails they wriggle,
And ghastly they glare on the face of the dead.
But the worst of all are the stars of whiteness,
That spill in a pool of pearly flame,
Pretty as gems in their silver brightness,
And etching a man for a bullet's aim.

Yet oh, it's great to be here with danger,
Here in the weird, death-pregnant dark,
In the devil's pasture a stealthy ranger,
When the moon is decently hiding. Hark!
What was that? Was it just the shiver
Of an eerie wind or a clammy hand?

The rustle of grass, or the passing quiver
Of one of the ghosts of No Man's Land?

It's only at night when the ghosts awaken,
And gibber and whisper horrible things;
For to every foot of this God-forsaken
Zone of jeopard some horror clings.
Ugh! What was that? It felt like a jelly,
That flattish mound in the noisome grass;
You three big rats running free of its belly,
Out of my way and let me pass!

But if there's horror, there's beauty, wonder;
The trench lights gleam and the rockets play.
That flood of magnificent orange yonder
Is a battery blazing miles away.
With a rush and a singing a great shell passes;
The rifles resentfully bicker and brawl,
And here I crouch in the dew-drenched grasses,
And look and listen and love it all.

God! What a life! But I must make haste now,
Before the shadow of night be spent.
It's little the time there is to waste now,
If I'd do the job for which I was sent.
My bombs are right and my clippers ready,
And I wriggle out to the chosen place,
When I hear a rustle . . . Steady! . . . Steady!
Who am I staring slap in the face?

There in the dark I can hear him breathing,
A foot away, and as still as death;

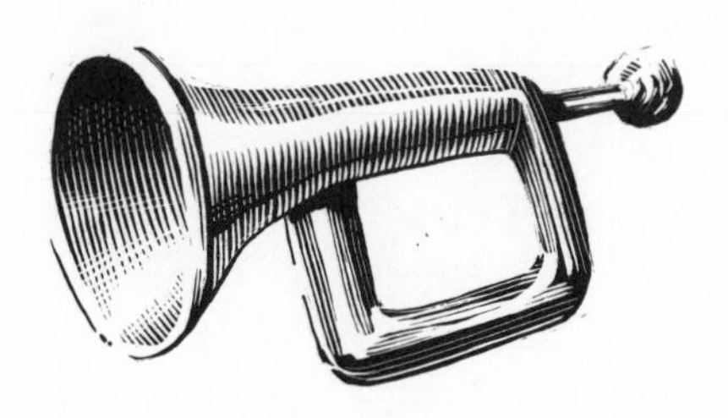

And my heart beats hard, and my brain is seething,
And I know he's a Hun by the smell of his breath.
Then: "Will you surrender?" I whisper hoarsely,
For it's death, swift death to utter a cry.
"English schwein-hund!" he murmurs coarsely.
"Then we'll fight it out in the dark," say I.

So we grip and we slip and we trip and wrestle
There in the gutter of No Man's Land;
And I feel my nails in his wind-pipe nestle,
And he tries to gouge, but I bite his hand.
And he tries to squeal, but I squeeze him tighter:
"Now," I say, "I can kill you fine;
But tell me first, you Teutonic blighter!
Have you any children?" He answers: "Nein."

Nine! Well, I cannot kill such a father,
So I tie his hands and I leave him there.
Do I finish my little job? Well, rather;
And I get home safe with some light to spare.
Heigh-ho! by day it's just prosy duty,
Doing the same old song and dance;
But oh! with the night—joy, glory, beauty:
Over the parapet—Life, Romance!

Carry On!

It's easy to fight when everything's right,
And you're mad with the thrill and the glory;
It's easy to cheer when victory's near,
And wallow in fields that are gory.
It's a different song when everything's wrong.
When you're feeling infernally mortal;
When it's ten against one, and hope there is none,
Buck up, little soldier and chortle:

Carry on! Carry on!
There isn't much punch in your blow.
You're glaring and staring and hitting out blind;
You're muddy and bloody, but never you mind.
Carry on! Carry on!
You haven't the ghost of a show.
It's looking like death, but while you've a breath,
Carry on, my son! Carry on!

And so in the strife of the battle of life
It's easy to fight when you're winning;
It's easy to slave, and starve and be brave,
When the dawn of success is beginning.
But the man who can meet despair and defeat
With a cheer, there's the man of God's choosing;
The man who can fight to Heaven's own height
Is the man who can fight when he's losing.

Carry on! Carry on!
Things never were looming so black.
But show that you haven't a cowardly streak,
And though you're unlucky you never are weak.

CARRY ON!

Carry on! Carry on!
Brace up for another attack.
It's looking like hell, but—you never can tell:
Carry on, old man! Carry on!

There are some who drift out in the deserts of doubt,
And some who in brutishness wallow;
There are others, I know, who in piety go
Because of a Heaven to follow.
But to labour with zest, and to give of your best,
For the sweetness and joy of the giving;
To help folks along with a hand and a song;
Why, there's the real sunshine of living.

Carry on! Carry on!
Fight the good fight and true;
Believe in your mission, greet life with a cheer;
There's big work to do, and that's why you are here.
Carry on! Carry on!
Let the world be the better for you;
And at last when you die, let this be your cry:
Carry on, my soul! Carry on!

The Baldness Of Chewed-Ear

When Chewed-ear Jenkins got hitched up to Guinneyveer McGee,
His flowin' locks, ye recollect, wuz frivolous an' free;
But in old Hymen's jack-pot, it's a most amazin' thing,
Them flowin' locks jest disappeared like snow-balls in the Spring;
Jest seemed to wilt an' fade away like dead leaves in the Fall,
An' left old Chewed-ear balder than a white-washed cannon ball.

Now Missis Chewed-ear Jenkins, that wuz Guinneyveer McGee,
Wuz jest about as fine a draw as ever made a pair;
But when the boys got joshin' an' suggested it was she
That must be inflooenshul for the old man's slump in hair—
Why! Missis Chewed-ear Jenkins jest went clean up in the air.

"To demonstrate," sez she that night, "the lovin' wife I am,
I've bought a dozen bottles of Bink's Anty-Dandruff Balm.
'Twill make yer hair jest sprout an' curl like squash-vines in the sun,
An' I'm propose to sling it on till every drop is done."
That hit old Chewed-ear's funny side, so he lays back an' hollers:
"The day you raise a hair, old girl, you'll git a thousand dollars."

Now, whether 'twas the prize or not 'tis mighty hard to say,
But Chewed-ear didn't seem to have much comfort from that day.

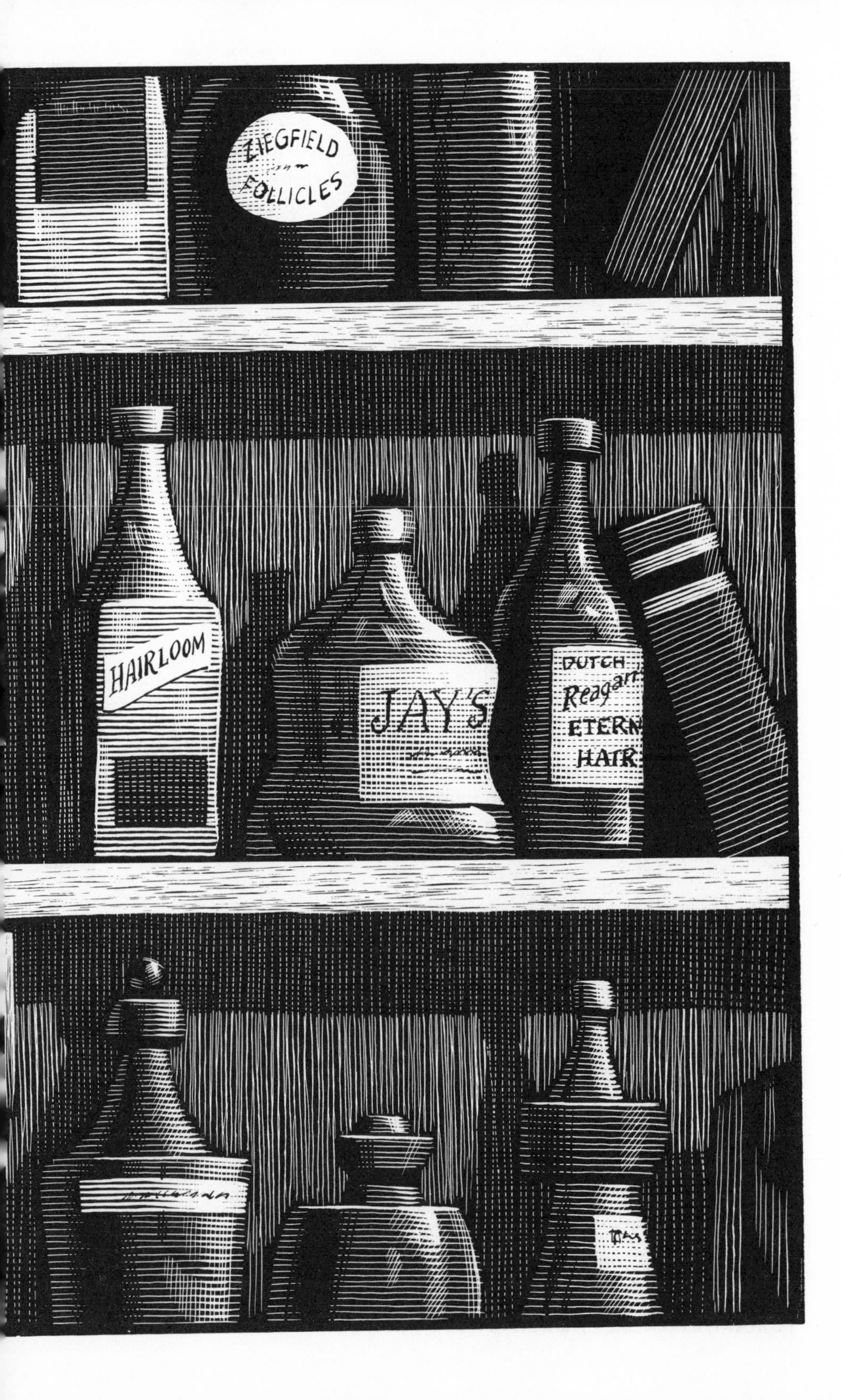
ZIEGFIELD
FOLLICLES
HAIRLOOM
JAY'S
DUTCH
HAIR

With bottles of that dandruff dope she followed at his heels,
An' sprinkled an' massaged him even when he ate his meals.
She waked him from his beauty sleep with tender, lovin' care,
An' rubbed an' scrubbed assiduous, yet never sign of hair.

Well, naturally all the boys soon tumbled to the joke,
An' at the Wow-wow's Social 'twas Cold-deck Davis spoke:
"The little woman's working mighty hard on Chewed-ear's crown;
Let's give her for a three-fifth's share a hundred dollars down
We stand to make five hundred clear—boys, drink in whiskey straight.
'The Chewed-ear Jenkins Hirsute Propagation Syndicate.' "

The boys wuz on, an' soon chipped in the necessary dust;
They primed up a committy to negotiate the deal;
Then Missis Jenkins yielded, bein' rather in disgust,
An' all wuz signed an' witnessed, an' invested with a seal.
They rounded up old Chewed-ear, an' they broke it what they'd done;
Allowed they'd bought an interest in his chance of raisin' hair;
They yanked his hat off anxiouslike, opinin' one by one
Their magnifyin' glasses showed fine prospects everywhere.
They bought Hairlene, an' Thatchem, an' Jay's Capillery Juice,
An' Seven Something Sisters, an' Macassar an' Bay Rum,
An' everyone insisted on his speshul right to sluice
His speshul line of lotion onto Chewed-ear's cranium.
They only got the merrier the more the old man roared,
An' shares in "Jenkins Hirsute" went sky-highin' on the board.

The Syndicate wuz hopeful that they'd demonstrate the pay,
An' Missis Jenkins laboured in her perseverin' way.
The boys discussed on "surface rights," an' "out-crops" an' so on,
An' planned to have it "crown" surveyed, an' blue prints of it drawn.
They ran a base line, sluiced an' yelled, an' everyone wuz glad,
Except the balance of the property, an' he wuz "mad."
"It gives me pain," he interjects, "to squash yer glowin' dream,
But you wuz fools when you got in on this here 'Hirsute' scheme.

You'll never raise a hair on me," when lo! that very night,
Preparin' to retire he got a most onpleasant fright:
For on that shinin' dome of his, so prominently bare,
He felt the baby outcrop of a second growth of hair.

A thousand dollars! Sufferin' Cæsar! Well, it must be saved!
He grabbed his razor recklesslike, an' shaved an' shaved an' shaved.
An' when his head was smooth again he gives a mighty sigh,
An' sneaks away, an' buys some Hair Destroyer on the sly.
So there wuz Missis Jenkins with "Restorer" wagin' fight,
An' Chewed-ear with "Destroyer" circumventin' her at night.
The battle wuz a mighty one; his nerves wuz on the strain,
An' yet in spite of all he did that hair began to gain.

The situation grew intense, so quietly one day,
He gave his share-holders the slip, an' made his get-a-way.
Jest like a criminal he skipped, an' aimed to defalcate
The Chewed-ear Jenkins Hirsute Propagation Syndicate.
His guilty secret burned him, an' he sought the city's din:
"I've got to get a wig," sez he, "to cover up my sin.
It's growin', growin' night an' day; it's most amazin' hair";
An' when he looked at it that night, he shuddered with despair.
He shuddered an' suppressed a cry at what his optics seen—
For on my word of honour, boys, that hair wuz growin' *green*.

At first he guessed he'd get some dye, an' try to dye it black;
An' then he saw 'twas Nemmysis wuz layin' on his track.
He must jest face the music, an' confess the thing he done,
An' pay the boys an' Guinneyveer the money they had won.
An' then there came a big idee—it thrilled him like a shock.
Why not control the Syndicate by buyin' up the Stock?

An' so next day he hurried back with smoothly shaven pate,
An' for a hundred dollars he bought up the Syndicate.
'Twas mighty frenzied finance an' the boys set up a roar,
But "Hirsutes" from the market wuz withdrawn for evermore.
An' to this day in Nuggetsville they tell the tale how slick
The Syndicate sold out too soon, and Chewed-ear turned the trick.

The Ballad Of The Brand

'Twas up in a land long famed for gold, where women were far and rare,
Tellus, the smith, had taken to wife a maiden amazingly fair;
Tellus, the brawny worker in iron, hairy and heavy of hand,
Saw her and loved her and bore her away from the tribe of a Southern land;
Deeming her worthy to queen his home and mother him little ones,
That the name of Tellus, the master smith, might live in his stalwart sons.

Now there was little of law in the land, and evil doings were rife,
And every man who joyed in his home guarded the fame of his wife.
For there were those of the silver tongue and the honeyed art to beguile,
Who would cozen the heart from a woman's breast and damn her soul with a smile.
And there were women too quick to heed a look or a whispered word,
And once in a while a man was slain, and the ire of the King was stirred;
So far and wide he proclaimed his wrath, and this was the law he willed:
"That whosoever killeth a man, even shall he be killed."

Now Tellus, the smith, he trusted his wife; his heart was empty of fear.
High on the hill was the gleam of their hearth, a beacon of love and cheer.

High on the hill they builded their bower, where the broom and the bracken meet;
Under a grave of oaks it was, hushed and drowsily sweet.
Here he enshrined her, his dearest saint, his idol, the light of his eye;
Her kisses rested upon his lips as brushes a butterfly.
The weight of her arms around his neck was light as the thistle down;
And sweetly she studied to win his smile, and gently she mocked his frown.
And when at the close of the dusty day his clangorous toil was done,
She hastened to meet him down the way all lit by the amber sun.

Their dove-cot gleamed in the golden light, a temple of stainless love;
Like the hanging cup of a big blue flower was the topaz sky above.
The roses and lilies yearned to her, as swift through their throng she pressed;
A little white, fragile, fluttering thing that lay like a child on his breast.
Then the heart of Tellus, the smith, was proud, and sang for the joy of life,
And there in the bronzing summertide he thanked the gods for his wife.

Now there was one called Philo, a scribe, a man of exquisite grace,
Carved like the god Apollo in limb, fair as Adonis in face:
Eager and winning of manner, full of such radiant charm,
Womenkind fought for his favor and loved to their uttermost harm.
Such was his craft and his knowledge, such was his skill at the game,
Never was woman could flout him, so be he plotted her shame.
And so he drank deep of pleasure, and then it fell on a day
He gazed on the wife of Tellus and marked her out for his prey.

Tellus, the smith, was merry, and the time of the year it was June,

So he said to his stalwart helpers: "Shut down the forge at noon.
Go ye and joy in the sunshine, rest in the coolth of the grove,
Drift on the dreamy river, every man with his love."
Then to himself: "Oh, Beloved, sweet will be your surprise;
To-day will we sport like children, laugh in each other's eyes;
Weave gay garlands of poppies, crown each other with flowers,
Pull plump carp from the lilies, rifle the ferny bowers.
To-day with feasting and gladness the wine of Cyprus will flow;
To-day is the day we were wedded only a twelve-month ago."

The larks trilled high in the heavens; his heart was lyric with joy;
He plucked a posy of lilies; he sped like a love-sick boy.
He stole up the velvety pathway—his cottage was sunsteeped
and still;
Vines honeysuckled the window; softly he peeped o'er the sill.
The lilies dropped from his fingers; devils were choking his
breath;
Rigid with horror, he stiffened; ghastly his face was as death.

Like a nun whose faith in the Virgin is met with a prurient jibe,
He shrank—'twas the wife of his bosom in the arms of Philo, the
scribe.

Tellus went back to his smithy; he reeled like a drunken man:
His heart was riven with anguish; his brain was brooding a plan.
Straight to his anvil he hurried; started his furnace aglow;
Heated his iron and shaped it with savage and masterful blow.
Sparks showered over and round him; swiftly under his hand
There at last it was finished—a hideous and infamous Brand.

That night the wife of his bosom, the light of joy in her eyes,
Kissed him with words of rapture; but he knew that her words
were lies.
Never was she so beguiling, never so merry of speech
(For passion ripens a woman as the sunshine ripens a peach).
He clenched his teeth into silence; he yielded up to her lure,
Though he knew that her breasts were heaving from the fire of
her paramour.
"To-morrow," he said, "to-morrow"—he wove her hair in a
strand,
Twisted it round his fingers and smiled as he thought of the
Brand.

The morrow was come, and Tellus swiftly stole up the hill.
Butterflies drowsed in the noon-heat; coverts were sunsteeped
and still.
Softly he padded the pathway unto the porch, and within
Heard he the low laugh of dalliance, heard he the rapture of sin.
Knew he her eyes were mystic with light that no man should see,
No man kindle and joy in, no man on earth save he.
And never for him would it kindle. The bloodlust surged in his
brain;
Through the senseless stone could he see them, wanton and
warily fain.
Horrible! Heaven he sought for, gained it and gloried and fell—
Oh, it was sudden—headlong into the nethermost hell. . . .

Was this he, Tellus, this marble? Tellus . . . not dreaming a
dream?
Ah! sharp-edged as a javelin, was that a woman's scream?

Was it a door that shattered, shell-like, under his blow?
Was it his saint, that strumpet, dishevelled and cowering low?
Was it her lover, that wild thing, that twisted and gouged and tore?
Was it a man he was crushing, whose head he beat on the floor?
Laughing the while at its weakness, till sudden he stayed his hand—
Through the red ring of his madness flamed the thought of the Brand.

Then bound he the naked Philo with thongs that cut in the flesh,
And the wife of his bosom, fear-frantic, he gagged with a silken mesh,
Choking her screams into silence; bound her down by the hair;
Dragged her lover unto her under her frenzied stare.
In the heat of the hearth-fire embers he heated the hideous Brand;
Twisting her fingers open, he forced its haft in her hand.
He pressed it downward and downward; she felt the living flesh sear;
She saw the throe of her lover; she heard the scream of his fear.
Once, twice and thrice he forced her, heedless of prayer and shriek—
Once on the forehead of Philo, twice in the soft of his cheek.
Then (for the thing was finished) he said to the woman: "See
How you have branded your lover! Now will I let him go free."
He severed the thongs that bound him, laughing: "Revenge is sweet,"
And Philo, sobbing in anguish, feebly rose to his feet.
The man who was fair as Apollo, god-like in woman's sight,
Hideous now as a satyr, fled to the pity of night.

Then came they before the Judgment Seat, and thus spoke the Lord of the Land:
"He who seeketh his neighbor's wife shall suffer the doom of the Brand.
Brutish and bold on his brow be it stamped, deep in his cheek let it sear,
That every man may look on his shame, and shudder and sicken and fear.

He shall hear their mock in the market-place, their fleering jibe at the feast;
He shall seek the caves and the shroud of night, and the fellowship of the beast.
Outcast forever from homes of men, far and far shall he roam.
Such be the doom, sadder than death, of him who shameth a home."

The World's All Right

Be honest, kindly, simple, true;
Seek good in all, scorn but pretence;
Whatever sorrow come to you,
Believe in Life's Beneficence!

The World's all right; serene I sit,
And cease to puzzle over it.
There's much that's mighty strange, no doubt;
But Nature knows what she's about;
And in a million years or so
We'll know more than to-day we know.
Old Evolution's under way—
What ho! the World's all right, I say.

Could things be other than they are?
All's in its place, from mote to star.
The thistledown that flits and flies
Could drift no hair-breadth otherwise.
What is, must be; with rhythmic laws
All Nature chimes, Effect and Cause.
The sand-grain and the sun obey—
What ho! the World's all right, I say.

Just try to get the Cosmic touch,
The sense that "you" don't matter much.
A million stars are in the sky;
A million planets plunge and die;
A million million men are sped;
A million million wait ahead.

Each plays his part and has his day—
What ho! the World's all right, I say.

Just try to get the Chemic view:
A million million lives made "you."
In lives a million you will be
Immortal down Eternity;
Immortal on this earth to range,
With never death, but ever change.
You always were, and will be aye—
What ho! the World's all right, I say.

Be glad! And do not blindly grope
For Truth that lies beyond our scope:
A sober plot informeth all
Of Life's uproarious carnival.
Your day is such a little one,
A gnat that lives from sun to sun;
Yet gnat and you have parts to play—
What ho! the World's all right, I say.

And though it's written from the start,
Just act your best your little part.
Just be as happy as you can,
And serve your kind, and die—a man.
Just live the good that in you lies,

And seek no guerdon of the skies;
Just make your Heaven here, to-day—
  What ho! the World's all right, I say.

Remember! in Creation's swing
The Race and not the man's the thing.
There's battle, murder, sudden death,
And pestilence, with poisoned breath.
Yet quick forgotten are such woes;
On, on the stream of Being flows.
Truth, Beauty, Love uphold their sway—
  What ho! the World's all right, I say.

The World's all right; serene I sit,
And joy that I am part of it;
And put my trust in Nature's plan,
And try to aid her all I can;
Content to pass, if in my place
I've served the uplift of the Race.
Truth! Beauty! Love! O Radiant Day—
  What ho! the World's all right, I say.

The Spell Of The Yukon

I wanted the gold, and I sought it;
  I scrabbled and mucked like a slave.
Was it famine or scurvy—I fought it;
  I hurled my youth into a grave.
I wanted the gold, and I got it—
  Came out with a fortune last fall,—
Yet somehow life's not what I thought it,
  And somehow the gold isn't all.

No! There's the land. (Have you seen it?)
  It's the cussedest land that I know,
From the big, dizzy mountains that screen it
  To the deep, deathlike valleys below.
Some say God was tired when He made it;
  Some say it's a fine land to shun;
Maybe; but there's some as would trade it
  For no land on earth—and I'm one.

You come to get rich (damned good reason);
  You feel like an exile at first;
You hate it like hell for a season,
  And then you are worse than the worst.
It grips you like some kinds of sinning;
  It twists you from foe to a friend;
It seems it's been since the beginning;
  It seems it will be to the end.

I've stood in some mighty-mouthed hollow
  That's plumb-full of hush to the brim;

I've watched the big, husky sun wallow
  In crimson and gold, and grow dim,
Till the moon set the pearly peaks gleaming,
  And the stars tumbled out, neck and crop;
And I've thought that I surely was dreaming,
  With the peace o' the world piled on top.

The summer—no sweeter was ever;
  The sunshiny woods all athrill;
The grayling aleap in the river,
  The bighorn asleep on the hill.
The strong life that never knows harness;
  The wilds where the caribou call;
The freshness, the freedom, the farness—
  O God! how I'm stuck on it all.

The winter! the brightness that blinds you,
  The white land locked tight as a drum,
The cold fear that follows and finds you,
  The silence that bludgeons you dumb.
The snows that are older than history,
  The woods where the weird shadows slant;
The stillness, the moonlight, the mystery,
  I've bade 'em good-by—but I can't.

There's a land where the mountains are nameless,
  And the rivers all run God knows where;
There are lives that are erring and aimless,
  And deaths that just hang by a hair;
There are hardships that nobody reckons;
  There are valleys unpeopled and still;
There's a land—oh, it beckons and beckons,
  And I want to go back—and I will.

They're making my money diminish;
  I'm sick of the taste of champagne.
Thank God! when I'm skinned to a finish
  I'll pike to the Yukon again.
I'll fight—and you bet it's no sham-fight;
  It's hell!—but I've been there before;

And it's better than this by a damsite—
  So me for the Yukon once more.

There's gold, and it's haunting and haunting;
  It's luring me on as of old;
Yet it isn't the gold that I'm wanting
  So much as just finding the gold.
It's the great, big, broad land 'way up yonder,
  It's the forests where silence has lease;
It's the beauty that thrills me with wonder,
  It's the stillness that fills me with peace.

The Pines

We sleep in the sleep of ages, the bleak, barbarian pines;
The gray moss drapes us like sages, and closer we lock our lines,
And deeper we clutch through the gelid gloom where never a
sunbeam shines.

On the flanks of the storm-gored ridges are our black battalions
massed;
We surge in a host to the sullen coast, and we sing in the ocean
blast;
From empire of sea to empire of snow we grip our empire fast.

To the niggard lands were we driven, 'twixt desert and floes are
we penned;
To us was the Northland given, ours to stronghold and defend;
Ours till the world be riven in the crash of the utter end;

Ours from the bleak beginning, through the æons of death-like
sleep;
Ours from the shock when the naked rock was hurled from the
hissing deep;
Ours through the twilight ages of weary glacier creep.

Wind of the East, Wind of the West, wandering to and fro,
Chant your songs in our topmost boughs, that the sons of men
may know
The peerless pine was the first to come, and the pine will be
last to go!

We pillar the halls of perfumed gloom; we plume where the
eagles soar;
The North-wind swoops from the brooding Pole, and our an-
cients crash and roar;

But where one falls from the crumbling walls shoots up a hardy
score.

We spring from the gloom of the canyon's womb; in the valley's
lap we lie;
From the white foam-fringe, where the breakers cringe, to the
peaks that tusk the sky,
We climb, and we peer in the crag-locked mere that gleams like
a golden eye.

Gain to the verge of the hog-back ridge where the vision ranges
free:
Pines and pines and the shadow of pines as far as the eye can see;
A steadfast legion of stalwart knights in dominant empery.

Sun, moon and stars give answer; shall we not staunchly stand,
Even as now, forever, wards of the wilder strand,
Sentinels of the stillness, lords of the last, lone land?

Dirt

Dirt is just matter out of place,
So scientists aver;
But when I see a miner's face
I wonder if they err.
For grit and grime and grease may be
In God's constructive plan,
A symbol of nobility,
The measure of a man.

There's nought so clean as honest dirt,
So of its worth I sing;
I value more an oily shirt
Than garment of a king.
There's nought so proud as honest sweat,
And though its stink we cuss,
We kid-glove chaps are in the debt
Of those who sweat for us.

It's dirt and sweat that makes us folks
Proud as we are today;
We owe our wealth to weary blokes
Befouled by soot and clay.
And where you see a belly fat
A dozen more are lean. . . .
By God! I'd sooner doff my hat
To washer-wife than queen.

So here's a song to dirt and sweat,
A grace to grit and grime;
A hail to workers who beget
The wonders of our time.

And as they gaze, though gutter-girt,
To palaces enskied,
Let them believe, by sweat and dirt,
They, too, are glorified.

The Shooting Of Dan McGrew

A bunch of the boys were whooping it up in the Malamute
saloon;
The kid that handles the music-box was hitting a jag-time tune;
Back of the bar, in a solo game, sat Dangerous Dan McGrew,
And watching his luck was his light-o'-love, the lady that's
known as Lou.

When out of the night, which was fifty below, and into the din
and the glare,
There stumbled a miner fresh from the creeks, dog-dirty, and
loaded for bear.
He looked like a man with a foot in the grave and scarcely the
strength of a louse,
Yet he tilted a poke of dust on the bar, and he called for drinks
for the house.
There was none could place the stranger's face, though we
searched ourselves for a clue;
But we drank his health, and the last to drink was Dangerous
Dan McGrew.

There's men that somehow just grip your eyes, and hold them
hard like a spell;
And such was he, and he looked to me like a man who had lived
in hell;
With a face most hair, and the dreary stare of a dog whose day
is done,
As he watered the green stuff in his glass, and the drops fell one
by one.
Then I got to figgering who he was, and wondering what he'd
do,

And I turned my head—and there watching him was the lady that's known as Lou.

His eyes went rubbering round the room, and he seemed in a kind of daze,
Till at last that old piano fell in the way of his wandering gaze.
The rag-time kid was having a drink; there was no one else on the stool,
So the stranger stumbles across the room, and flops down there like a fool.
In a buckskin shirt that was glazed with dirt he sat, and I saw him sway;
Then he clutched the keys with his talon hands—my God! but that man could play.

Were you ever out in the Great Alone, when the moon was awful clear,
And the icy mountains hemmed you in with a silence you most could *hear;*
With only the howl of a timber wolf, and you camped there in the cold,
A half-dead thing in a stark, dead world, clean mad for the muck called gold;
While high overhead, green, yellow and red, the North Lights swept in bars?—
Then you've a hunch what the music meant . . . hunger and night and the stars.

And hunger not of the belly kind, that's banished with bacon and beans,
But the gnawing hunger of lonely men for a home and all that it means;
For a fireside far from the cares that are, four walls and a roof above;
But oh! so cramful of cosy joy, and crowned with a woman's love—
A woman dearer than all the world, and true as Heaven is true—
(God! how ghastly she looks through her rouge,—the lady that's known as Lou.)

MALA
Sal

Then on a sudden the music changed, so soft that you scarce could hear;
But you felt that your life had been looted clean of all that it once held dear;
That someone had stolen the woman you loved; that her love was a devil's lie;
That your guts were gone, and the best for you was to crawl away and die.
'Twas the crowning cry of a heart's despair, and it thrilled you through and through—
"I guess I'll make it a spread misere," said Dangerous Dan McGrew.

The music almost died away . . . then it burst like a pent-up flood;
And it seemed to say, "Repay, repay," and my eyes were blind with blood.
The thought came back of an ancient wrong, and it stung like a frozen lash,
And the lust awoke to kill, to kill . . . then the music stopped with a crash,
And the stranger turned, and his eyes they burned in a most peculiar way;
In a buckskin shirt that was glazed with dirt he sat, and I saw him sway;
Then his lips went in in a kind of grin, and he spoke, and his voice was calm,
And "Boys," says he, "you don't know me, and none of you care a damn;
But I want to state, and my words are straight, and I'll bet my poke they're true,
That one of you is a hound of hell . . . and that one is Dan McGrew."

Then I ducked my head, and the lights went out, and two guns blazed in the dark,
And a woman screamed, and the lights went up, and two men lay stiff and stark.
Pitched on his head, and pumped full of lead, was Dangerous Dan McGrew,

While the man from the creeks lay clutched to the breast of the lady that's known as Lou.

These are the simple facts of the case, and I guess I ought to know.
They say that the stranger was crazed with "hooch," and I'm not denying it's so.
I'm not so wise as the lawyer guys, but strictly between us two—
The woman that kissed him and—pinched his poke—was the lady that's known as Lou.

The Wedding Ring

I pawned my sick wife's wedding ring,
To drink and make myself a beast.
I got the most that it would bring,
Of golden coins the very least.
With stealth into her room I crept
And stole it from her as she slept.

I do not think that she will know,
As in its place I left a band
Of brass that has a brighter glow
And gleamed upon her withered hand.
I do not think that she can tell
The change—she does not see too well.

Pray God, she doesn't find me out.
I'd rather far I would be dead.
Yet yesterday she seemed to doubt,
And looking at me long she said:
"My finger must have shrunk, because
My ring seems bigger than it was."

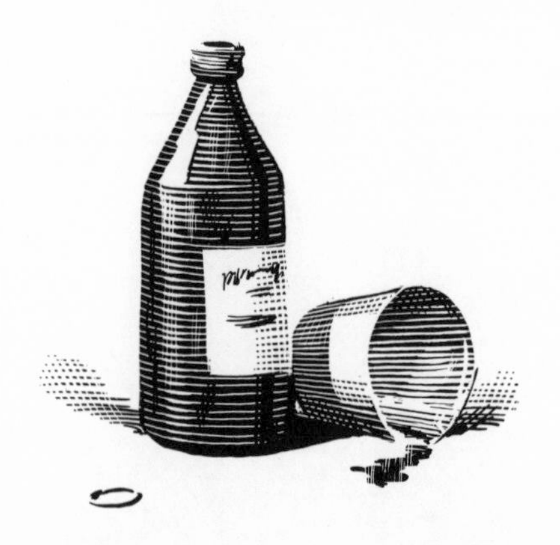

She gazed at it so wistfully,
And one big tear rolled down her cheek.
Said she: "You'll bury it with me . . ."
I was so moved I could not speak.
Oh wretched me! How whisky can
Bring out the devil in a man!

And yet I know she loves me still,
As on the morn that we were wed;
And darkly guess I also will
Be doomed the day that she is dead.
And yet I swear, before she's gone,
I will retrieve her ring from pawn.

I'll get it though I have to steal,
Then when to ease her bitter pain
They give her sleep oh I will feel
Her hand and slip it on again;
Through tears her wasted face I'll see,
And pray to God: "Oh pity me!"

Barb-Wire Bill

At dawn of day the white land lay all gruesome-like and grim,
When Bill Mc'Gee he says to me: "We've *got* to do it, Jim.
"We've got to make Fort Liard quick. I know the river's bad,
"But, oh! the little woman's sick . . . why! don't you savvy, lad?"
And me! Well, yes, I must confess it wasn't hard to see
Their little family group of two would soon be one of three.
And so I answered, careless-like: "Why, Bill! you don't suppose
"I'm scared of that there 'babbling brook'? Whatever you say—goes."

A real live man was Barb-wire Bill, with insides copperlined;
For "barb-wire" was the brand of "hooch" to which he most inclined.
They knew him far; his igloos are on Kittiegazuit strand.
They knew him well, the tribes who dwell within the Barren Land.
From Koyokuk to Kuskoquim his fame was everywhere;
And he did love, all life above, that little Julie Claire,
The lithe, white slave-girl he had bought for seven hundred skins,
And taken to his wickiup to make his moccasins.

We crawled down to the river bank and feeble folk were we,
That Julie Claire from God-knows-where, and Barb-wire Bill and me.
From shore to shore we heard the roar the heaving ice-floes make,
And loud we laughed, and launched our raft, and followed in their wake.
The river swept and seethed and leapt, and caught us in its stride;

And on we hurled amid a world that crashed on every side.
With sullen din the banks caved in; the shore-ice lanced the stream;
The naked floes like spooks arose, all jiggling and agleam.
Black anchor-ice of strange device shot upward from its bed,
As night and day we cleft our way, and arrow-like we sped.

But "Faster still!" cried Barb-wire Bill, and looked the live-long day
In dull despair at Julie Claire, as white like death she lay.
And sometimes he would seem to pray and sometimes seem to curse,
And bent above, with eyes of love, yet ever she grew worse.
And as we plunged and leapt and lunged, her face was plucked with pain,
And I could feel his nerves of steel a-quiver at the strain.
And in the night he gripped me tight as I lay fast asleep:
"The river's kicking like a steer . . . run out the forward sweep!
"That's Hell-gate Canyon right ahead; I know of old its roar,
"And . . . I'll be damned! *the ice is jammed!* We've *got* to make the shore."

With one wild leap I gripped the sweep. The night was black as sin.
The float-ice crashed and ripped and smashed, and stunned us with its din.
And near and near, and clear and clear I heard the canyon boom;
And swift and strong we swept along to meet our awful doom.
And as with dread I glimpsed ahead the death that waited there,
My only thought was of the girl, the little Julie Claire;
And so, like demon mad with fear, I panted at the oar,
And foot by foot, and inch by inch, we worked the raft ashore.

The bank was staked with grinding ice, and as we scraped and crashed,
I only knew one thing to do, and through my mind it flashed:
Yet while I groped to find the rope, I heard Bill's savage cry:
"That's my job, lad! It's me that jumps. I'll snub this raft or die!"
I saw him leap, I saw him creep, I saw him gain the land;
I saw him crawl, I saw him fall, then run with rope in hand.

And then the darkness gulped him up, and down we dashed once
more,
And nearer, nearer drew the jam, and thunder-like its roar.

Oh God! all's lost . . . from Julie Claire there came a wail of
pain,
And then—the rope grew sudden taut, and quivered at the strain;
It slacked and slipped, it whined and gripped, and oh, I held my
breath!
And there we hung and there we swung right in the jaws of
death.

A little strand of hempen rope, and how I watched it there,
With all around a hell of sound, and darkness and despair;
A little strand of hempen rope, I watched it all alone,
And somewhere in the dark behind I heard a woman moan;
And somewhere in the dark ahead I heard a man cry out,
Then silence, silence, silence fell, and mocked my hollow shout.
And yet once more from out the shore I heard that cry of pain,
A moan of mortal agony, then all was still again.

That night was hell with all the frills, and when the dawn broke
dim,
I saw a lean and level land, but never sign of him.
I saw a flat and frozen shore of hideous device,
I saw a long-drawn strand of rope that vanished through the ice.
And on that treeless, rockless shore I found my partner—dead.
No place was there to snub the raft, so—*he had served instead;*
And with the rope lashed round his waist, in last defiant fight,
He'd thrown himself beneath the ice, that closed and gripped
him tight;
And there he'd held us back from death, as fast in death he
lay. . . .
Say, boys! I'm not the pious brand, but—I just tried to pray.
And then I looked to Julie Claire, and sore abashed was I,
For from the robes that covered her, *I—heard—a—baby—
cry. . . .*

Thus was Love conqueror of death, and life for life was given;
And though no saint on earth, d'ye think—Bill's squared hisself
with Heaven?

The Lunger

Jack would laugh an' joke all day;
Never saw a lad so gay;
Singin' like a medder lark,
Loaded to the Plimsoll mark
With God's sunshine was that boy;
Had a strangle-holt on Joy.
Held his head 'way up in air,
Left no callin' cards on Care;
Breezy, buoyant, brave and true;
Sent his sunshine out to you;
Cheerfulest when clouds was black—
    Happy Jack! Oh, Happy Jack!

Sittin' in my shack alone
I could hear him in his own,
Singin' far into the night,
Till it didn't seem just right
One man should corral the fun,
Live his life so in the sun;
Didn't seem quite natural
Not to have a grouch at all;
Not a trouble, not a lack—
    Happy Jack! Oh, Happy Jack!

He was plumbful of good cheer
Till he struck that low-down year;
Got so thin, so little to him,
You could most see day-light through him.
Never was his eye so bright,
Never was his cheek so white.
Seemed as if somethin' was wrong,

Sort o' quaver in his song.
Same old smile, same hearty voice:
"Bless you, boys! let's all rejoice!"
But old Doctor shook his head:
"Half a lung," was all he said.
Yet that half was surely right,
For I heard him every night,
Singin', singin' in his shack—
    Happy Jack! Oh, Happy Jack!

Then one day a letter came
Endin' with a female name;
Seemed to get him in the neck,
Sort o' pile-driver effect;
Paled his lip and plucked his breath,
Left him starin' still as death.
Somethin' had gone awful wrong,
Yet that night he sang his song.
Oh, but it was good to hear!
For there clutched my heart a fear,
So that I quaked listenin'
Every night to hear him sing.
But each day he laughed with me,
An' his smile was full of glee.
Nothin' seemed to set him back—
    Happy Jack! Oh, Happy Jack!

Then one night the singin' stopped . . .
Seemed as if my heart just flopped;
For I'd learned to love the boy
With his gilt-edged line of joy,
With his glorious gift of bluff,
With his splendid fightin' stuff.
Sing on, lad, and play the game!
O dear God! . . . no singin' came,
But there surged to me instead—
Silence, silence, deep and dread;
Till I shuddered, tried to pray.
Said: "He's maybe gone away."

Oh, yes, he had gone away,
Gone forever and a day.
But he'd left behind him there,
In his cabin, pinched and bare,
His poor body, skin and bone,
His sharp face, cold as a stone.
An' his stiffened fingers pressed
Somethin' bright upon his breast:
Locket with a silken curl,
Poor, sweet portrait of a girl.
Yet I reckon at the last
How defiant-like he passed;
For there sat upon his lips
Smile that death could not eclipse;
An' within his eyes lived still
Joy that dyin' could not kill.

An' now when the nights are long,
How I miss his cheery song!
How I sigh an' wish him back!
    Happy Jack! Oh, Happy Jack!

Dreams Are Best

I just think that dreams are best,
Just to sit and fancy things;
Give your gold no acid test,
Try not how your silver rings;
Fancy women pure and good,
Fancy men upright and true:
Fortressed in your solitude,
Let Life be a dream to you.

For I think that Thought is all;
Truth's a minion of the mind;
Love's ideal comes at call;
As ye seek so shall ye find.
But ye must not seek too far;
Things are never what they seem:
Let a star be just a star,
And a woman—just a dream.

O you Dreamers, proud and pure,
You have gleaned the sweet of life!
Golden truths that shall endure
Over pain and doubt and strife.
I would rather be a fool
Living in my Paradise,
Than the leader of a school,
Sadly sane and weary wise.

O you Cynics with your sneers,
Fallen brains and hearts of brass,
Tweak me by my foolish ears,
Write me down a simple ass!
I'll believe the real "you"

Is the "you" without a taint;
I'll believe each woman too,
But a slightly damaged saint.

Yes, I'll smoke my cigarette,
Vestured in my garb of dreams,
And I'll borrow no regret;
All is gold that golden gleams.
So I'll charm my solitude
With the faith that Life is blest,
Brave and noble, bright and good, . . .
Oh, I think that dreams are best!

My Friends

The man above was a murderer, the man below was a thief,
And I lay there in the bunk between, ailing beyond belief,
A weary armful of skin and bone, wasted with pain and grief.

My feet were froze, and the lifeless toes were purple and green
and gray;
The little flesh that clung to my bones, you could punch it in
holes like clay;
The skin on my gums was a sullen black, and slowly peeling
away.

I was sure enough in a direful fix, and often I wondered why
They did not take the chance that was left and leave me alone
to die,
Or finish me off with a dose of dope—so utterly lost was I.

But no; they brewed me the green-spruce tea, and nursed me
there like a child;
And the homicide he was good to me, and bathed my sores and
smiled;
And the thief he starved that I might be fed, and his eyes were
kind and mild.

Yet they were woefully wicked men, and often at night in pain
I heard the murderer speak of his deed and dream it over again;
I heard the poor thief sorrowing for the dead self he had slain.

I'll never forget that bitter dawn, so evil, askew and gray,
When they wrapped me round in the skins of beasts and they
bore me to a sleigh,
And we started out with the nearest post an hundred miles away.

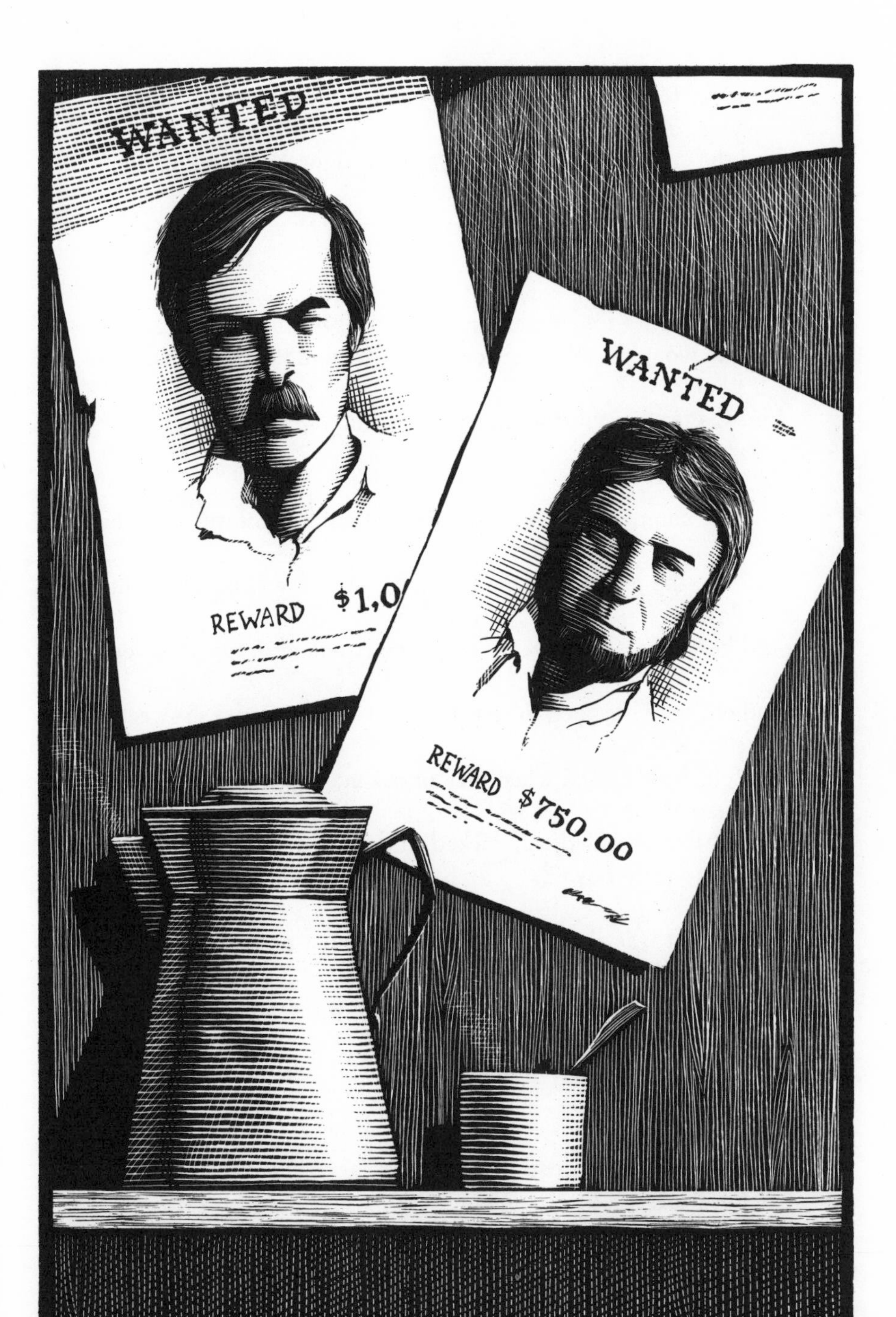
WANTED
REWARD $1,0
WANTED
REWARD $750.00

I'll never forget the trail they broke, with its tense, unuttered woe;
And the crunch, crunch, crunch as their snowshoes sank through the crust of the hollow snow;
And my breath would fail, and every beat of my heart was like a blow.

And oftentimes I would die the death, yet wake up to life anew;
The sun would be all ablaze on the waste, and the sky a blighting blue,
And the tears would rise in my snow-blind eyes and furrow my cheeks like dew.

And the camps we made when their strength outplayed and the day was pinched and wan;
And oh, the joy of that blessed halt, and how I did dread the dawn;
And how I hated the weary men who rose and dragged me on.

And oh, how I begged to rest, to rest—the snow was so sweet a shroud;
And oh, how I cried when they urged me on, cried and cursed them aloud;
Yet on they strained, all racked and pained, and sorely their backs were bowed.

And then it was all like a lurid dream, and I prayed for a swift release
From the ruthless ones who would not leave me to die alone in peace;
Till I wakened up and I found myself at the post of the Mounted Police.

And there was my friend the murderer, and there was my friend the thief,
With bracelets of steel around their wrists, and wicked beyond belief:
But when they come to God's judgment seat—may I be allowed the brief.

The Song Of The Soldier-Born

Give me the scorn of the stars and a peak defiant;
Wail of the pines and a wind with the shout of a giant;
Night and a trail unknown and a heart reliant.

Give me to live and love in the old, bold fashion;
A soldier's billet at night and a soldier's ration;
A heart that leaps to the fight with a soldier's passion.

For I hold as a simple faith there's no denying;
The trade of a soldier's the only trade worth plying;
The death of a soldier's the only death worth dying.

So let me go and leave your safety behind me;
Go to the spaces of hazard where nothing shall bind me;
Go till the word is War—and then you will find me.

Then you will call me and claim me because you will need me;
Cheer me and gird me and into the battle-wrath speed me. . . .
And when it's over, spurn me and no longer heed me.

For guile and a purse gold-greased are the arms you carry;
With deeds of paper you fight and with pens you parry;
You call on the hounds of the law your foes to harry.

You with your "Art for its own sake," posing and prinking;
You with your "Live and be merry," eating and drinking;
You with your "Peace at all hazard," from bright blood shrink-
ing.

Fools! I will tell you now: though the red rain patters,
And a million of men go down, it's little it matters. . . .
There's the Flag upflung to the stars, though it streams in tatters.

There's a glory gold never can buy to yearn and to cry for;
There's a hope that's as old as the sky to suffer and sigh for;
There's a faith that out-dazzles the sun to martyr and die for.

Ah no! it's my dream that War will never be ended;
That men will perish like men, and valour be splendid;
That the Flag by the sword will be served, and honour defended.

That the tale of my fights will never be ancient story;
That though my eye may be dim and my beard be hoary,
I'll die as a soldier dies on the Field of Glory.

So give me a strong right arm for a wrong's swift righting;
Stave of a song on my lips as my sword is smiting;
Death in my boots may-be, but fighting, fighting.

The Trail Of Ninety-Eight

I

Gold! We leapt from our benches. Gold! We sprang from our stools.
Gold! We wheeled in the furrow, fired with the faith of fools.
Fearless, unfound, unfitted, far from the night and the cold,
Heard we the clarion summons, followed the master-lure—Gold!

Men from the sands of the Sunland; men from the woods of the West;
Men from the farms and the cities, into the Northland we pressed.
Graybeards and striplings and women, good men and bad men and bold,
Leaving our homes and our loved ones, crying exultantly—"Gold!"

Never was seen such an army, pitiful, futile, unfit;
Never was seen such a spirit, manifold courage and grit.
Never has been such a cohort under one banner unrolled
As surged to the ragged-edged Arctic, urged by the arch-tempter—Gold.

"Farewell!" we cried to our dearests; little we cared for their tears.
"Farewell!" we cried to the humdrum and the yoke of the hireling years;
Just like a pack of school-boys, and the big crowd cheered us good-bye.
Never were hearts so uplifted, never were hopes so high.

The spectral shores flitted past us, and every whirl of the screw
Hurled us nearer to fortune, and ever we planned what we'd
do—
Do with the gold when we got it—big, shiny nuggets like plums,
There in the sand of the river, gouging it out with our thumbs.

And one man wanted a castle, another a racing stud;
A third would cruise in a palace yacht like a red-necked prince
of blood.
And so we dreamed and we vaunted, millionaires to a man,
Leaping to wealth in our visions long ere the trail began.

II

We landed in wind-swept Skagway. We joined the weltering
mass,
Clamoring over their outfits, waiting to climb the Pass.
We tightened our girths and our pack-straps; we linked on the
Human Chain,
Struggling up to the summit, where every step was a pain.

Gone was the joy of our faces, grim and haggard and pale;
The heedless mirth of the shipboard was changed to the care of
the trail.
We flung ourselves in the struggle, packing our grub in relays,
Step by step to the summit in the bale of the winter days.

Floundering deep in the sump-holes, stumbling out again;
Crying with cold and weakness, crazy with fear and pain.
Then from the depths of our travail, ere our spirits were broke,
Grim, tenacious and savage, the lust of the trail awoke.

"Klondike or bust!" rang the slogan; every man for his own.
Oh, how we flogged the horses, staggering skin and bone!
Oh, how we cursed their weakness, anguish they could not tell,
Breaking their hearts in our passion, lashing them on till they
fell!

For grub meant gold to our thinking, and all that could walk
must pack;

The sheep for the shambles stumbled, each with a load on its back;
And even the swine were burdened, and grunted and squealed and rolled,
And men went mad in the moment, huskily clamoring "Gold!"

Oh, we were brutes and devils, goaded by lust and fear!
Our eyes were strained to the summit; the weaklings dropped to the rear,
Falling in heaps by the trail-side, heart-broken, limp and wan;
But the gaps closed up in an instant, and heedless the chain went on.

Never will I forget it, there on the mountain face,
Antlike, men with their burdens, clinging in icy space;
Dogged, determined and dauntless, cruel and callous and cold,
Cursing, blaspheming, reviling, and ever that battle-cry—"Gold!"

Thus toiled we, the army of fortune, in hunger and hope and despair,
Till glacier, mountain and forest vanished, and, radiantly fair,
There at our feet lay Lake Bennett, and down to its welcome we ran:
The trail of the land was over, the trail of the water began.

III

We built our boats and we launched them. Never has been such a fleet;
A packing-case for a bottom, a mackinaw for a sheet.
Shapeless, grotesque, lopsided, flimsy, makeshift and crude,
Each man after his fashion builded as best he could.

Each man worked like a demon, as prow to rudder we raced;
The winds of the Wild cried "Hurry!" the voice of the waters, "Haste!"
We hated those driving before us; we dreaded those pressing behind;

We cursed the slow current that bore us; we prayed to the God
of the wind.

Spring! and the hillsides flourished, vivid in jewelled green;
Spring! and our hearts' blood nourished envy and hatred and
spleen.
Little cared we for the Spring-birth; much cared we to get on—
Stake in the Great White Channel, stake ere the best be gone.

The greed of the gold possessed us; pity and love were forgot;
Covetous visions obsessed us; brother with brother fought.
Partner with partner wrangled, each one claiming his due;
Wrangled and halved their outfits, sawing their boats in two.

Thuswise we voyaged Lake Bennett, Tagish, then Windy Arm,
Sinister, savage and baleful, boding us hate and harm.
Many a scow was shattered there on that iron shore;
Many a heart was broken straining at sweep and oar.

We roused Lake Marsh with a chorus, we drifted many a mile;
There was the canyon before us—cave-like its dark defile;
The shores swept faster and faster; the river narrowed to wrath;
Waters that hissed disaster reared upright in our path.

Beneath us the green tumult churning, above us the cavernous
gloom;
Around us, swift twisting and turning, the black, sullen walls of
a tomb.
We spun like a chip in a mill-race; our hearts hammered under
the test;
Then—oh, the relief on each chill face!—we soared into sun-
light and rest.

Hand sought for hand on the instant. Cried we, "Our troubles
are o'er!"
Then, like a rumble of thunder, heard we a canorous roar.
Leaping and boiling and seething, saw we a cauldron afume;
There was the rage of the rapids, there was the menace of doom.

The river springs like a racer, sweeps through a gash in the
rock;

Butts at the boulder-ribbed bottom, staggers and rears at the shock;
Leaps like a terrified monster, writhes in its fury and pain;
Then with the crash of a demon springs to the onset again.

Dared we that ravening terror; heard we its din in our ears;
Called on the Gods of our fathers, juggled forlorn with our fears;
Sank to our waists in its fury, tossed to the sky like a fleece;
Then, when our dread was the greatest, crashed into safety and peace.

But what of the others that followed, losing their boats by the score?
Well could we see them and hear them, strung down that desolate shore.
What of the poor souls that perished? Little of them shall be said—
On to the Golden Valley, pause not to bury the dead.

Then there were days of drifting, breezes soft as a sigh;
Night trailed her robe of jewels over the floor of the sky.
The moonlit stream was a python, silver, sinuous, vast,
That writhed on a shroud of velvet—well, it was done at last.

There were the tents of Dawson, there the scar of the slide;
Swiftly we poled o'er the shallows, swiftly leapt o'er the side.
Fires fringed the mouth of Bonanza; sunset gilded the dome;
The test of the trail was over—thank God, thank God, we were Home!

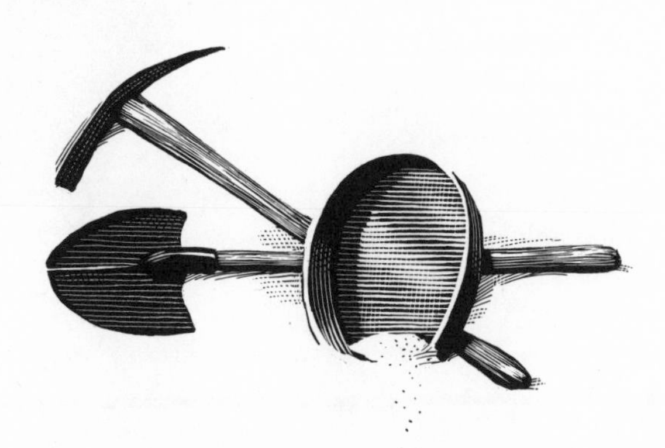

The Quitter

When you're lost in the Wild, and you're scared as a child,
  And Death looks you bang in the eye,
And you're sore as a boil, it's according to Hoyle
  To cock your revolver and . . . die.
But the Code of a Man says: "Fight all you can,"
  And self-dissolution is barred.
In hunger and woe, oh, it's easy to blow . . .
  It's the hell-served-for-breakfast that's hard.

"You're sick of the game!" Well, now, that's a shame.
  You're young and you're brave and you're bright.
"You've had a raw deal!" I know—but don't squeal,
  Buck up, do your damnedest, and fight.
It's the plugging away that will win you the day,
  So don't be a piker, old pard!
Just draw on your grit; it's so easy to quit:
  It's the keeping-your-chin-up that's hard.

It's easy to cry that you're beaten—and die;
  It's easy to crawfish and crawl;
But to fight and to fight when hope's out of sight—
  Why, that's the best game of them all!
And though you come out of each gruelling bout,
  All broken and beaten and scarred,
Just have one more try—it's dead easy to die,
  It's the keeping-on-living that's hard.

Clancy Of The Mounted Police

In the little Crimson Manual it's written plain and clear
That who would wear the scarlet coat shall say good-bye to fear;
Shall be a guardian of the right, a sleuth-hound of the trail—
In the little Crimson Manual there's no such word as "fail"—
Shall follow on though heavens fall, or hell's top-turrets freeze,
Half round the world, if need there be, on bleeding hands and knees.
It's duty, duty, first and last, the Crimson Manual saith;
The Scarlet Rider makes reply: "It's duty—to the death."
And so they sweep the solitudes, free men from all the earth;
And so they sentinel the woods, the wilds that know their worth;
And so they scour the startled plains and mock at hurt and pain,
And read their Crimson Manual, and find their duty plain.
Knights of the lists of unrenown, born of the frontier's need,
Disdainful of the spoken word, exultant in the deed;
Unconscious heroes of the waste, proud players of the game,
Props of the power behind the throne, upholders of the name:
For thus the Great White Chief hath said, "In all my lands be peace,"
And to maintain his word he gave his West the Scarlet Police.

Livid-lipped was the valley, still as the grave of God;
Misty shadows of mountain thinned into mists of cloud;
Corpselike and stark was the land, with a quiet that crushed and awed,
And the stars of the weird sub-arctic glimmered over its shroud.

Deep in the trench of the valley two men stationed the Post,
Seymour and Clancy the reckless, fresh from the long patrol;
Seymour, the sergeant, and Clancy—Clancy who made his boast
He could cinch like a bronco the Northland, and cling to the prongs of the Pole.

Two lone men on detachment, standing for law on the trail;
Undismayed in the vastness, wise with the wisdom of old—
Out of the night hailed a half-breed telling a pitiful tale,
"White man starving and crazy on the banks of the Nordenscold."

Up sprang the red-haired Clancy, lean and eager of eye;
Loaded the long toboggan, strapped each dog at its post;
Whirled his lash at the leader; then, with a whoop and a cry,
Into the Great White Silence faded away like a ghost.

The clouds were a misty shadow, the hills were a shadowy mist;
Sunless, voiceless and pulseless, the day was a dream of woe;
Through the ice-rifts the river smoked and bubbled and hissed;
Behind was a trail fresh broken, in front the untrodden snow.

Ahead of the dogs ploughed Clancy, haloed by steaming breath;
Through peril of open water, through ache of insensate cold;
Up rivers wantonly winding in a land affianced to death,
Till he came to a cowering cabin on the banks of the Nordenscold.

Then Clancy loosed his revolver, and he strode through the open door;
And there was the man he sought for, crouching beside the fire;
The hair of his beard was singeing, the frost on his back was hoar,
And ever he crooned and chanted as if he never would tire:—

"I panned and I panned in the shiny sand, and I sniped on the river bar;
But I know, I know, that it's down below that the golden treasures are;

So I'll wait and wait till the floods abate, and I'll sink a shaft once more,
And I'd like to bet that I'll go home yet with a brass band playing before."

He was nigh as thin as a sliver, and he whined like a Moose-hide cur;
So Clancy clothed him and nursed him as a mother nurses a child;
Lifted him on the toboggan, wrapped him in robes of fur,
Then with the dogs sore straining started to face the Wild.

Said the Wild, "I will crush this Clancy, so fearless and insolent;
For him will I loose my fury, and blind and buffet and beat;
Pile up my snows to stay him; then when his strength is spent,
Leap on him from my ambush and crush him under my feet.

"Him will I ring with my silence, compass him with my cold;
Closer and closer clutch him unto mine icy breast;
Buffet him with my blizzards, deep in my snows enfold,
Claiming his life as my tribute, giving my wolves the rest."

Clancy crawled through the vastness; o'er him the hate of the Wild;
Full on his face fell the blizzard; cheering his huskies he ran;
Fighting, fierce-hearted and tireless, snows that drifted and piled,
With ever and ever behind him singing the crazy man.

"Sing hey, sing ho, for the ice and snow,
And a heart that's ever merry;
Let us trim and square with a lover's care
(For why should a man be sorry?)
A grave deep, deep, with the moon a-peep,
A grave in the frozen mould.
Sing hey, sing ho, for the winds that blow,
And a grave deep down in the ice and snow,
A grave in the land of gold."

Day after day of darkness, the whirl of the seething snows;
Day after day of blindness, the swoop of the stinging blast;

On through a blur of fury the swing of staggering blows;
  On through a world of turmoil, empty, inane and vast.

Night with its writhing storm-whirl, night despairingly black;
  Night with its hours of terror, numb and endlessly long;
Night with its weary waiting, fighting the shadows back.
  And ever the crouching madman singing his crazy song.

Cold with its creeping terror, cold with its sudden clinch;
  Cold so utter you wonder if 'twill ever again be warm;
Clancy grinned as he shuddered, "Surely it isn't a cinch
  Being wet-nurse to a loony in the teeth of an arctic storm."

The blizzard passed and the dawn broke, knife-edged and crystal clear;
  The sky was a blue-domed iceberg, sunshine outlawed away;
Ever by snowslide and ice-rip haunted and hovered the Fear;
  Ever the Wild malignant poised and panted to slay.

The lead-dog freezes in harness—cut him out of the team!
  The lung of the wheel-dog's bleeding—shoot him and let him lie!
On and on with the others—lash them until they scream!
  "Pull for your lives, you devils! On! To halt is to die."

There in the frozen vastness Clancy fought with his foes;
  The ache of the stiffened fingers, the cut of the snowshoe thong;
Cheeks black-raw through the hood-flap, eyes that tingled and closed,
  And ever to urge and cheer him quavered the madman's song.

Colder it grew and colder, till the last heat left the earth,
  And there in the great stark stillness the balefires glinted and gleamed,
And the Wild all around exulted and shook with a devilish mirth,
  And life was far and forgotten, the ghost of a joy once dreamed.

Death! And one who defied it, a man of the Mounted Police;
  Fought it there to a standstill long after hope was gone;

Grinned through his bitter anguish, fought without let or cease,
Suffering, straining, striving, stumbling, struggling on.

Till the dogs lay down in their traces, and rose and staggered and fell;
Till the eyes of him dimmed with shadows, and the trail was so hard to see;
Till the Wild howled out triumphant, and the world was a frozen hell—
Then said Constable Clancy: "I guess that it's up to me."

Far down the trail they saw him, and his hands they were blanched like bone;
His face was a blackened horror, from his eyelids the salt rheum ran;
His feet he was lifting strangely, as if they were made of stone,
But safe in his arms and sleeping he carried the crazy man.

So Clancy got into Barracks, and the boys made rather a scene;
And the O. C. called him a hero, and was nice as a man could be;
But Clancy gazed down his trousers at the place where his toes had been,
And then he howled like a husky, and sang in a shaky key.

"When I go back to the old love that's true to the finger-tips,
I'll say: 'Here's bushels of gold, love,' and I'll kiss my girl on the lips;
'It's yours to have and to hold, love.' It's the proud, proud boy I'll be,
When I go back to the old love that's waited so long for me."

Young Fellow My Lad

"Where are you going, Young Fellow My Lad,
On this glittering morn of May?"
"I'm going to join the Colours, Dad;
They're looking for men, they say."
"But you're only a boy, Young Fellow My Lad;
You aren't obliged to go."
"I'm seventeen and a quarter, Dad,
And ever so strong, you know."

. . . .

"So you're off to France, Young Fellow My Lad,
And you're looking so fit and bright."
"I'm terribly sorry to leave you, Dad,
But I feel that I'm doing right."
"God bless you and keep you, Young Fellow My Lad,
You're all of my life, you know."
"Don't worry. I'll soon be back, dear Dad,
And I'm awfully proud to go."

. . . .

"Why don't you write, Young Fellow My Lad?
I watch for the post each day;
And I miss you so, and I'm awfully sad,
And it's months since you went away.
And I've had the fire in the parlour lit,
And I'm keeping it burning bright
Till my boy comes home; and here I sit
Into the quiet night."

. . . .

"What is the matter, Young Fellow My Lad?
No letter again to-day.

Why did the postman look so sad,
And sigh as he turned away?
I hear them tell that we've gained new ground,
But a terrible price we've paid:
God grant, my boy, that you're safe and sound;
But oh I'm afraid, afraid."

. . . .

"They've told me the truth, Young Fellow My Lad:
You'll never come back again:
(Oh God! the dreams and the dreams I've had,
And the hopes I've nursed in vain!)
For you passed in the night, Young Fellow My Lad,
And you proved in the cruel test
Of the screaming shell and the battle hell
That my boy was one of the best.

"So you'll live, you'll live, Young Fellow My Lad,
In the gleam of the evening star,
In the wood-note wild and the laugh of the child,
In all sweet things that are.
And you'll never die, my wonderful boy,
While life is noble and true;
For all our beauty and hope and joy
We will owe to our lads like you."

The Cremation Of Sam McGee

There are strange things done in the midnight sun
By the men who moil for gold;
The Arctic trails have their secret tales
That would make your blood run cold;
The Northern Lights have seen queer sights,
But the queerest they ever did see
Was that night on the marge of Lake Lebarge
I cremated Sam McGee.

Now Sam McGee was from Tennessee, where the cotton blooms and blows.
Why he left his home in the South to roam 'round the Pole, God only knows.
He was always cold, but the land of gold seemed to hold him like a spell;
Though he'd often say in his homely way that "he'd sooner live in hell."

On a Christmas Day we were mushing our way over the Dawson trail.
Talk of your cold! through the parka's fold it stabbed like a driven nail.
If our eyes we'd close, then the lashes froze till sometimes we couldn't see;
It wasn't much fun, but the only one to whimper was Sam McGee.

And that very night, as we lay packed tight in our robes beneath the snow,

And the dogs were fed, and the stars o'erhead were dancing heel and toe,
He turned to me, and "Cap," says he, "I'll cash in this trip, I guess;
And if I do, I'm asking that you won't refuse my last request."

Well, he seemed so low that I couldn't say no; then he says with a sort of moan:
"It's the cursèd cold, and it's got right hold till I'm chilled clean through to the bone.
Yet 'tain't being dead—it's my awful dread of the icy grave that pains;
So I want you to swear that, foul or fair, you'll cremate my last remains."

A pal's last need is a thing to heed, so I swore I would not fail;
And we started on at the streak of dawn; but God! he looked ghastly pale.
He crouched on the sleigh, and he raved all day of his home in Tennessee;
And before nightfall a corpse was all that was left of Sam McGee.

There wasn't a breath in that land of death, and I hurried, horror-driven,
With a corpse half hid that I couldn't get rid, because of a promise given;
It was lashed to the sleigh, and it seemed to say: "You may tax your brawn and brains,
But you promised true, and it's up to you to cremate those last remains."

Now a promise made is a debt unpaid, and the trail has its own stern code.
In the days to come, though my lips were dumb, in my heart how I cursed that load.
In the long, long night, by the lone firelight, while the huskies, round in a ring,
Howled out their woes to the homeless snows— O God! how I loathed the thing.

And every day that quiet clay seemed to heavy and heavier grow;
And on I went, though the dogs were spent and the grub was getting low;
The trail was bad, and I felt half mad, but I swore I would not give in;
And I'd often sing to the hateful thing, and it hearkened with a grin.

Till I came to the marge of Lake Lebarge, and a derelict there lay;
It was jammed in the ice, but I saw in a trice it was called the "Alice May."
And I looked at it, and I thought a bit, and I looked at my frozen chum;
Then "Here," said I, with a sudden cry, "is my cre-ma-tor-eum."

Some planks I tore from the cabin floor, and I lit the boiler fire;
Some coal I found that was lying around, and I heaped the fuel higher;
The flames just soared, and the furnace roared—such a blaze you seldom see;
And I burrowed a hole in the glowing coal, and I stuffed in Sam McGee.

Then I made a hike, for I didn't like to hear him sizzle so;
And the heavens scowled, and the huskies howled, and the wind began to blow.
It was icy cold, but the hot sweat rolled down my cheeks, and I don't know why;
And the greasy smoke in an inky cloak went streaking down the sky.

I do not know how long in the snow I wrestled with grisly fear;
But the stars came out and they danced about ere again I ventured near;
I was sick with dread, but I bravely said: "I'll just take a peep inside.
I guess he's cooked, and it's time I looked"; . . . then the door I opened wide.

And there sat Sam, looking cool and calm, in the heart of the furnace roar;
And he wore a smile you could see a mile, and he said: "Please close that door.
It's fine in here, but I greatly fear you'll let in the cold and storm—
Since I left Plumtree, down in Tennessee, it's the first time I've been warm."

There are strange things done in the midnight sun
By the men who moil for gold;
The Arctic trails have their secret tales
That would make your blood run cold;
The Northern Lights have seen queer sights,
But the queerest they ever did see
Was that night on the marge of Lake Lebarge
I cremated Sam McGee.

The Reckoning

It's fine to have a blow-out in a fancy restaurant,
With terrapin and canvas-back and all the wine you want;
To enjoy the flowers and music, watch the pretty women pass,
Smoke a choice cigar, and sip the wealthy water in your glass.
It's bully in a high-toned joint to eat and drink your fill,
But it's quite another matter when you
Pay the bill.

It's great to go out every night on fun or pleasure bent;
To wear your glad rags always and to never save a cent;
To drift along regardless, have a good time every trip;
To hit the high spots sometimes, and to let your chances slip;
To know you're acting foolish, yet to go on fooling still,
Till Nature calls a show-down, and you
Pay the bill.

Time has got a little bill—get wise while yet you may,
For the debit side's increasing in a most alarming way;

The things you had no right to do, the things you should have
done,
They're all put down; it's up to you to pay for every one.
So eat, drink and be merry, have a good time if you will,
But God help you when the time comes, and you
Foot the bill.

The Men That Don't Fit In

There's a race of men that don't fit in,
  A race that can't stay still;
So they break the hearts of kith and kin,
  And they roam the world at will.
They range the field and they rove the flood,
  And they climb the mountain's crest;
Theirs is the curse of the gypsy blood,
  And they don't know how to rest.

If they just went straight they might go far;
  They are strong and brave and true;
But they're always tired of the things that are,
  And they want the strange and new.
They say: "Could I find my proper groove,
  What a deep mark I would make!"
So they chop and change, and each fresh move
  Is only a fresh mistake.

And each forgets, as he strips and runs
  With a brilliant, fitful pace,
It's the steady, quiet, plodding ones
  Who win in the lifelong race.
And each forgets that his youth has fled,
  Forgets that his prime is past,
Till he stands one day, with a hope that's dead,
  In the glare of the truth at last.

He has failed, he has failed; he has missed his chance;
  He has just done things by half.

Life's been a jolly good joke on him,
  And now is the time to laugh.
Ha, ha! He is one of the Legion Lost;
  He was never meant to win;
He's a rolling stone, and it's bred in the bone;
  He's a man who won't fit in.

"?"

If you had the choice of two women to wed,
(Though of course the idea is quite absurd)
And the first from her heels to her dainty head
Was charming in every sense of the word:
And yet in the past (I grieve to state),
She never had been exactly "straight."

And the second—she was beyond all cavil,
A model of virtue, I must confess;
And yet, alas! she was dull as the devil,
And rather a dowd in the way of dress;
Though what she was lacking in wit and beauty,
She more than made up for in "sense of duty."

Now, suppose you must wed, and make no blunder,
And either would love you, and let you win her—
Which of the two would you choose, I wonder,
The stolid saint or the sparkling sinner?

The Call

(France, August first, 1914)

Far and near, high and clear,
Hark to the call of War!
Over the gorse and the golden dells,
Ringing and swinging of clamorous bells,
Praying and saying of wild farewells:
War! War! War!

High and low, all must go:
Hark to the shout of War!
Leave to the women the harvest yield;
Gird ye, men, for the sinister field;
A sabre instead of a scythe to wield:
War! Red War!

Rich and poor, lord and boor,
Hark to the blast of War!
Tinker and tailor and millionaire,
Actor in triumph and priest in prayer,
Comrades now in the hell out there,
Sweep to the fire of War!

Prince and page, sot and sage,
Hark to the roar of War!
Poet, professor and circus clown,
Chimney-sweeper and fop o' the town,
Into the pot and be melted down:
Into the pot of War!

Women all, hear the call,
The pitiless call of War!

Look your last on your dearest ones,
Brothers and husbands, fathers, sons:
Swift they go to the ravenous guns,
    The gluttonous guns of War.

    Everywhere thrill the air
    The maniac bells of War.
There will be little of sleeping to-night;
There will be wailing and weeping to-night;
Death's red sickle is reaping to-night:
    War! War! War!

The Twins

There were two brothers, John and James,
And when the town went up in flames,
To save the house of James dashed John,
Then turned, and lo! his own was gone.

And when the great World War began,
To volunteer John promptly ran;
And while he learned live bombs to lob,
James stayed at home and—sneaked his job.

John came home with a missing limb;
That didn't seem to worry him;
But oh, it set his brain awhirl
To find that James had—sneaked his girl!

Time passed. John tried his grief to drown;
To-day James owns one-half the town;
His army contracts riches yield;
And John? Well, *search the Potter's Field.*

LECT
ME
MAY

I Believe

It's my belief that every man
  Should do his share of work,
And in our economic plan
  No citizen should shirk.
That in return each one should get
  His meed of fold and food,
And feel that all his toil and sweat
  Is for the common good.

It's my belief that every chap
  Should have an equal start,
And there should be no handicap
  To hinder his depart;
That there be fairness in the fight,
  And justice in the race,
And every lad should have the right
  To win his proper place.

It's my belief that people should
  Be neither rich nor poor;
That none should suffer servitude,
  And all should be secure.
That wealth is loot, and rank is rot,
  And foul is class and clan;
That to succeed a man may not
  Exploit his brother man.

It's my belief that heritage
  And usury are wrong;
That each should win a worthy wage
  And sing an honest song. . . .

I BELIEVE

Not one like this—for though I rue
The wrong of life, I flout it.
Alas! I'm not prepared to do
A goddam thing about it.

The Ballad Of Pious Pete

"The North has got him."—Yukonism.

I tried to refine that neighbor of mine, honest to God, I did.
I grieved for his fate, and early and late I watched over him like a kid.
I gave him excuse, I bore his abuse in every way that I could;
I swore to prevail; I camped on his trail; I plotted and planned for his good.
By day and by night I strove in men's sight to gather him into the fold,
With precept and prayer, with hope and despair, in hunger and hardship and cold.
I followed him into Gehennas of sin, I sat where the sirens sit;
In the shade of the Pole, for the sake of his soul, I strove with the powers of the Pit.
I shadowed him down to the scrofulous town; I dragged him from dissolute brawls;
But I killed the galoot when he started to shoot electricity into my walls.

God knows what I did he should seek to be rid of one who would save him from shame.
God knows what I bore that night when he swore and bade me make tracks from his claim.
I started to tell of the horrors of hell, when sudden his eyes lit like coals;
And "Chuck it," says he, "don't persecute me with your cant and your saving of souls."
I'll swear I was mild as I'd be with a child, but he called me the son of a slut;

And, grabbing his gun with a leap and a run, he threatened my face with the butt.
So what could I do (I leave it to you)? With curses he harried me forth;
Then he was alone, and I was alone, and over us menaced the North.

Our cabins were near; I could see, I could hear; but between us there rippled the creek;
And all summer through, with a rancor that grew, he would pass me and never would speak.
Then a shuddery breath like the coming of Death crept down from the peaks far away;
The water was still; the twilight was chill; the sky was a tatter of gray.
Swift came the Big Cold, and opal and gold the lights of the witches arose;
The frost-tyrant clinched, and the valley was cinched by the stark and cadaverous snows.
The trees were like lace where the star-beams could chase, each leaf was a jewel agleam.
The soft white hush lapped the Northland and wrapped us round in a crystalline dream;
So still I could hear quite loud in my ear the swish of the pinions of time;
So bright I could see, as plain as could be, the wings of God's angels ashine.

As I read in the Book I would oftentimes look to that cabin just over the creek.
Ah me, it was sad and evil and bad, two neighbors who never would speak!
I knew that full well like a devil in hell he was hatching out, early and late,
A system to bear through the frost-spangled air the warm, crimson waves of his hate.
I only could peer and shudder and fear—'twas ever so ghastly and still;
But I knew over there in his lonely despair he was plotting me terrible ill.

I knew that he nursed a malice accurst, like the blast of a winnowing flame;
I pleaded aloud for a shield, for a shroud— Oh, God! then calamity came.

Mad! If I'm mad then you too are mad; but it's all in the point of view.
If you'd looked at them things gallivantin' on wings, all purple and green and blue;
If you'd noticed them twist, as they mounted and hissed like scorpions dim in the dark;
If you'd seen them rebound with a horrible sound, and spitefully spitting a spark;
If you'd watched *It* with dread, as it hissed by your bed, that thing with the feelers that crawls—
You'd have settled the brute that attempted to shoot electricity into your walls.

Oh, some they were blue, and they slithered right through; they were silent and squashy and round;
And some they were green; they were wriggly and lean; they writhed with so hateful a sound.
My blood seemed to freeze; I fell on my knees; my face was a white splash of dread.
Oh, the Green and the Blue, they were gruesome to view; but the worst of them all were the Red.
They came through the door, they came through the floor, they came through the moss-creviced logs.
They were savage and dire; they were whiskered with fire; they bickered like malamute dogs.
They ravined in rings like iniquitous things; they gulped down the Green and the Blue.
I crinkled with fear whene'er they drew near, and nearer and nearer they drew.

And then came the crown of Horror's grim crown, the monster so loathsomely red.
Each eye was a pin that shot out and in, as, squidlike, it oozed to my bed;
So softly it crept with feelers that swept and quivered like fine copper wire;

Its belly was white with a sulphurous light, its jaws were a-drooling with fire.
It came and it came; I could breathe of its flame, but never a wink could I look.
I thrust in its maw the Fount of the Law; I fended it off with the Book.
I was weak—oh, so weak—but I thrilled at its shriek, as wildly it fled in the night;
And deathlike I lay till the dawn of the day. (Was ever so welcome the light?)

I loaded my gun at the rise of the sun; to his cabin so softly I slunk.
My neighbor was there in the frost-freighted air, all wrapped in a robe in his bunk.
It muffled his moans; it outlined his bones, as feebly he twisted about;
His gums were so black, and his lips seemed to crack, and his teeth all were loosening out.
'Twas a death's head that peered through the tangle of beard; 'twas a face I will never forget;
Sunk eyes full of woe, and they troubled me so with their pleadings and anguish, and yet
As I rested my gaze in a misty amaze on the scurvy-degenerate wreck,
I thought of the Things with the dragon-fly wings, then laid I my gun on his neck.
He gave out a cry that was faint as a sigh, like a perishing malamute,
And he says unto me, "I'm converted," says he; "for Christ's sake, Peter, don't shoot!"

. . . .

They're taking me out with an escort about, and under a sergeant's care;
I am humbled indeed, for I'm 'cuffed to a Swede that thinks he's a millionaire.
But it's all Gospel true what I'm telling to you—up there where the Shadow falls—
That I settled Sam Noot when he started to shoot electricity into my walls.

Death In The Arctic

I

I took the clock down from the shelf;
"At eight," said I, "I shoot myself."
It lacked a *minute* of the hour,
And as I waited all a-cower,
A skinful of black, boding pain,
Bits of my life came back again. . . .

"Mother, there's nothing more to eat—
Why don't you go out on the street?
Always you sit and cry and cry;
Here at my play I wonder why.
Mother, when you dress up at night,
Red are your cheeks, your eyes are bright:
Twining a ribband in your hair,
Kissing good-bye you go down-stair
Then I'm as lonely as can be.
Oh, how I wish you were with me!
Yet when you go out on the street,
Mother, there's always lots to eat. . . . "

II

For days the igloo has been dark;
But now the rag wick sends a spark
That glitters in the icy air,
And wakes frost sapphires everywhere;
Bright, bitter flames, that adder-like
Dart here and there, yet fear to strike

The gruesome gloom wherein *they* lie,
My comrades, oh, so keen to die!
And I, the last—well, here I wait
The clock to strike the hour of eight. . . .

"Boy, it is bitter to be hurled
Nameless and naked on the world;
Frozen by night and starved by day,
Curses and kicks and clouts your pay.
But you must fight! Boy, look on me!
Anarch of all earth-misery;
Beggar and tramp and shameless sot;
Emblem of ill, in rags that rot.
Would you be foul and base as I?
Oh, it is better far to die!
Swear to me now you'll fight and fight,
Boy, or I'll kill you here to-night. . . . "

III

Curse this silence soft and black!
Sting, little light, the shadows back!
Dance, little flame, with freakish glee!
Twinkle with brilliant mockery!
Glitter on ice-robed roof and floor!
Jewel the bear-skin of the door!
Gleam in my beard, illume my breath,
Blanch the clock face that times my death!
But do not pierce that murk so deep,
Where in their sleeping-bags they sleep!
But do not linger where they lie,
They who had all the luck to die! . . .

"There is nothing more to say;
Let us part and go our way.
Since it seems we can't agree,
I will go across the sea.
Proud of heart and strong am I;
Not for woman will I sigh;
Hold my head up gay and glad:
You can find another lad. . . . "

GENEVA N. M.

IV

Above the igloo piteous flies
Our frayed flag to the frozen skies.
Oh, would you know how earth can be
A hell—go north of Eighty-three!
Go, scan the snows day after day,
And hope for help, and pray and pray;
Have seal-hide and sea-lice to eat;
Melt water with your body's heat;
Sleep all the fell, black winter through
Beside the dear, dead men you knew.
(The walrus blubber flares and gleams—
O God! how long a minute seems!) . . .

"*Mary, many a day has passed,*
Since that morn of hot-head youth.
Come I back at last, at last,
Crushed with knowing of the truth;
How through bitter, barren years
You loved me, and me alone;
Waited, wearied, wept your tears—
Oh, could I atone, atone,
I would pay a million-fold!
Pay you for the love you gave.
Mary, look down as of old—
I am kneeling by your grave." . . .

V

Olaf, the Blonde, was first to go;
Bitten his eyes were by the snow;
Sightless and sealed his eyes of blue,
So that he died before I knew.
Here in those poor weak arms he died:
"Wolves will not get you, lad," I lied;
"For I will watch till Spring come round;
Slumber you shall beneath the ground."
Oh, how I lied! I scarce can wait:
Strike, little clock, the hour of eight! . . .

"Comrade, can you blame me quite?
The horror of the long, long night
Is on me, and I've borne with pain
So long, and hoped for help in vain.
So frail am I, and blind and dazed;
With scurvy sick, with silence crazed.
Beneath the Arctic's heel of hate,
Avid for Death I wait, I wait.
Oh if I falter, fail to fight,
Can you, dear comrade, blame me quite?" . . .

VI

Big Eric gave up months ago.
But seldom do men suffer so.
His feet sloughed off, his fingers died,
His hands shrunk up and mummified.
I had to feed him like a child;
Yet he was valiant, joked and smiled,
Talked of his wife and little one
(Thanks be to God that I have none),
Passed in the night without a moan,
Passed, and I'm here, alone, alone. . . .

"I've got to kill you, Dick.
Your life for mine, you know.
Better to do it quick,
A swift and sudden blow.
See! here's my hand to lick;
A hug before you go—
God! but it makes me sick:
Old dog, I love you so.
Forgive, forgive me, Dick—
A swift and sudden blow. . . . "

VII

Often I start up in the dark,
Thinking the sound of bells to hear.
Often I wake from sleep. "Oh, hark!
Help . . . it is coming . . . near and near."

Blindly I reel toward the door;
There the snow billows bleak and bare;
Blindly I seek my den once more,
Silence and darkness and despair.
Oh, it is all a dreadful dream!
Scurvy and cold and death and dearth;
I will awake to warmth and gleam,
Silvery seas and greening earth.
Life is a dream, its wakening,
Death, gentle shadow of God's wing. . . .

"Tick, little clock, my life away!
Even a second seems a day.
Even a minute seems a year,
Peopled with ghosts, that press and peer
Into my face so charnel white,
Lit by the devilish, dancing light.
Tick, little clock! mete out my fate:
Tortured and tense I wait, I wait. . . ."

VIII

Oh, I have sworn! the hour is nigh:
When it strikes eight, I die, I die.
Raise up the gun—it stings my brow—
When it strikes eight . . . all ready . . . *now*—
. . . .

Down from my hand the weapon dropped;
Wildly I stared. . . .
THE CLOCK HAD STOPPED.

IX

Phantoms and fears and ghosts have gone.
Peace seems to nestle in my brain.
Lo! the clock stopped, I'm living on;
Heart-sick I was, and less than sane.
Yet do I scorn the thing I planned,
Hearing a voice: "O coward, fight!"
Then the clock stopped . . . whose was the hand?

Maybe 'twas God's—ah well, all's right.
Heap on me darkness, fold on fold!
Pain! wrench and rack me! What care I?
Leap on me, hunger, thirst and cold!
I will await my time to die;
Looking to Heaven that shines above;
Looking to God, and love . . . and love.

X

Hark! what is that? Bells, dogs again!
Is it a dream? I sob and cry.
See! the door opens, fur-clad men
Rush to my rescue; frail am I;
Feeble and dying, dazed and glad.
There is the pistol where it dropped.
"Boys, it was hard—but I'm not mad. . . .
Look at the clock—it stopped, it stopped.
Carry me out. The heavens smile.
See! there's an arch of gold above.
Now, let me rest a little while—
Looking to God and love . . . and love. . . . "

The Trapper's Christmas Eve

It's mighty lonesome-like and drear.
Above the Wild the moon rides high,
And shows up sharp and needle-clear
The emptiness of earth and sky;
No happy homes with love a-glow;
No Santa Claus to make believe:
Just snow and snow, and then more snow;
It's Christmas Eve, it's Christmas Eve.

And here am I where all things end,
And Undesirables are hurled;
A poor old man without a friend,
Forgot and dead to all the world;
Clean out of sight and out of mind . . .
Well, maybe it is better so;
We all in life our level find,
And mine, I guess, is pretty low.

Yet as I sit with pipe alight
Beside the cabin-fire, it's queer
This mind of mine must take to-night
The backward trail of fifty year.
The school-house and the Christmas tree;
The children with their cheeks a-glow;
Two bright blue eyes that smile on me . . .
Just half a century ago.

Again (it's maybe forty years),
With faith and trust almost divine,

These same blue eyes, abrim with tears,
Through depths of love look into mine.
A parting, tender, soft and low,
With arms that cling and lips that cleave . . .
Ah me! it's all so long ago,
Yet seems so sweet this Christmas Eve.

Just thirty years ago, again . . .
We say a bitter, *last* good-bye;
Our lips are white with wrath and pain;
Our little children cling and cry.
Whose was the fault? it matters not,
For man and woman both deceive;
It's buried now and all forgot,
Forgiven, too, this Christmas Eve.

And she (God pity me) is dead;
Our children men and women grown.
I like to think that they are wed,
With little children of their own,
That crowd around their Christmas tree . . .
I would not ever have them grieve,
Or shed a single tear for me,
To mar their joy this Christmas Eve.

Stripped to the buff and gaunt and still
Lies all the land in grim distress.
Like lost soul wailing, long and shrill,
A wolf-howl cleaves the emptiness.
Then hushed as Death is everything.
The moon rides haggard and forlorn . . .
"O hark the herald angels sing!"
God bless all men—it's Christmas morn.

The Dreamer

The lone man gazed and gazed upon his gold,
His sweat, his blood, the wage of weary days;
But now how sweet, how doubly sweet to hold
All gay and gleamy to the camp-fire blaze.
The evening sky was sinister and cold;
The willows shivered, wanly lay the snow;
The uncommiserating land, so old,
So worn, so grey, so niggard in its woe,
Peered through its ragged shroud. The lone man sighed,
Poured back the gaudy dust into its poke,
Gazed at the seething river listless-eyed,
Loaded his corn-cob pipe as if to smoke;
Then crushed with weariness and hardship crept
Into his ragged robe, and swiftly slept.

. . . .

Hour after hour went by; a shadow slipped
From vasts of shadow to the camp-fire flame;
Gripping a rifle with a deadly aim,
A gaunt and hairy man with wolfish eyes . . .

. . . .

The sleeper dreamed, and lo! this was his dream:
He rode a streaming horse across a moor.
Sudden 'mid pit-black night a lightning gleam
Showed him a way-side inn, forlorn and poor.
A sullen host unbarred the creaking door,
And led him to a dim and dreary room;
Wherein he sat and poked the fire a-roar,
So that weird shadows jigged athwart the gloom.
He ordered wine. 'Od's blood! but he was tired.
What matter! Charles was crushed and George was King,
His party high in power; but he aspired!
Red guineas packed his purse, too tight to ring.

The fire-light gleamed upon his silken hose,
His silver buckles and his powdered wig.
What ho! more wine! He drank, he slowly rose.
What made the shadows dance that madcap jig?
He clutched the candle, steered his way to bed,
And in a trice was sleeping like the dead.

. . . .

Across the room there crept, so shadow soft,
His sullen host, with naked knife a-gleam,
(A gaunt and hairy man with wolfish eyes.) . . .
And as he lay, the sleeper dreamed a dream.

. . . .

'Twas in a ruder land, a wilder day.
A rival princeling sat upon his throne,
Within a dungeon, dark and foul he lay,
With chains that bit and festered to the bone.
They haled him harshly to a vaulted room,
Where One gazed on him with malignant eye;
And in that devil-face he read his doom,
Knowing that ere the dawn-light he must die.
Well, he was sorrow-glutted; let them bring
Their prize assassins to the bloody work.
His kingdom lost, yet would he die a King,
Fearless and proud, as when he faced the Turk.
Ah God! the glory of that great Crusade!
The bannered pomp, the gleam, the splendid urge!
The crash of reeking combat, blade to blade!
The reeling ranks, blood-avid and a-surge!
For long he thought; then feeling o'er him creep
Vast weariness, he fell into a sleep.

. . . .

The cell door opened; soft the headsman came,
Within his hand a mighty axe a-gleam,
(A gaunt and hairy man with wolfish eyes,) . . .
And as he lay, the sleeper dreamed a dream.

. . . .

'Twas in a land unkempt of life's red dawn;
Where in his sanded cave he dwelt alone;
Sleeping by day, or sometimes worked upon
His flint-head arrows and his knives of stone;

By night stole forth and slew the savage boar,
So that he loomed a hunter of loud fame,
And many a skin of wolf and wild-cat wore,
And counted many a flint-head to his name;
Wherefore he walked the envy of the band,
Hated and feared, but matchless in his skill.
Till lo! one night deep in that shaggy land,
He tracked a yearling bear and made his kill;
Then over-worn he rested by a stream,
And sank into a sleep too deep for dream.

. . . .

Hunting his food a rival caveman crept
Through those dark woods, and marked him where he lay;
Cowered and crawled upon him as he slept,
Poising a mighty stone aloft to slay—
(A gaunt and hairy man with wolfish eyes.) . . .

. . . .

The great stone crashed. The Dreamer shrieked and woke,
And saw, fear-blinded, in his dripping cell,
A gaunt and hairy man, who with one stroke
Swung a great axe of steel that flashed and fell . . .

So that he woke amid his bedroom gloom,
And saw, hair-poised, a naked, thirsting knife,
A gaunt and hairy man with eyes of doom—
And then the blade plunged down to drink his life . . .
So that he woke, wrenched back his robe, and looked,
And saw beside his dying fire upstart
A gaunt and hairy man with finger crooked—
A rifle rang, a bullet searched his heart . . .

. . . .

The morning sky was sinister and cold.
Grotesque the Dreamer sprawled, and did not rise.
For long and long there gazed upon some gold
A gaunt and hairy man with wolfish eyes.

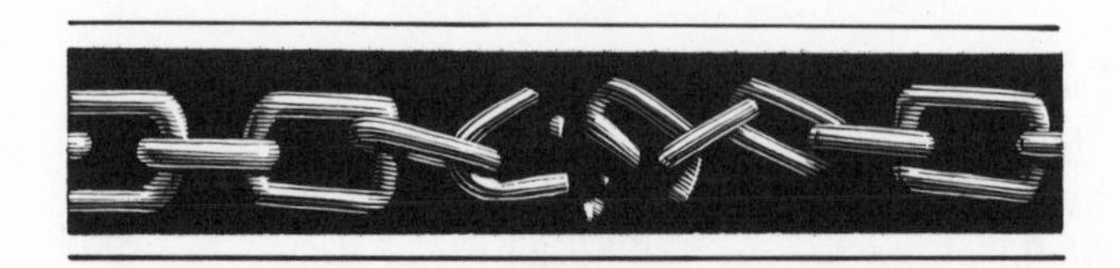

Bill The Bomber

The poppies gleamed like bloody pools through cotton-woolly mist;
The Captain kept a-lookin' at the watch upon his wrist;
And there we smoked and squatted, as we watched the shrapnel flame;
'Twas wonnerful, I'm tellin' you, how fast them bullets came.
'Twas weary work the waiting, though; I tried to sleep a wink,
For waitin' means a-thinkin', and it doesn't do to think.
So I closed my eyes a little, and I had a niceish dream
Of a-standin' by a dresser with a dish of Devon cream;
But I hadn't time to sample it, for suddenlike I woke:
"Come on, me lads!" the Captain says, 'n I climbed out through the smoke.

We spread out in the open: it was like a bath of lead;
But the boys they cheered and hollered fit to raise the bloody dead,
Till a beastly bullet copped 'em, then they lay without a sound,
And it's odd—we didn't seem to heed them corpses on the ground.
And I kept on thinkin', thinkin', as the bullets faster flew,
How they picks the werry best men, and they lets the rotters through;
So indiscriminatin' like, they spares a man of sin,
And a rare lad wot's a husband and a father gets done in.
And while havin' these reflections and advancin' on the run,
A bullet biffs me shoulder, and says I: "That's number one."

Well, it downed me for a jiffy, but I didn't lose me calm,
For I knew that I was needed: I'm a bomber, so I am.
I 'ad lost me cap and rifle, but I "carried on" because
I 'ad me bombs and knew that they was needed, so they was.

We didn't 'ave no singin' now, nor many men to cheer;
Maybe the shrapnel drowned 'em, crashin' out so werry near;
And the Maxims got us sideways, and the bullets faster flew,
And I copped one on me flipper, and says I: "That's number
two."

I was pleased it was the left one, for I 'ad me bombs, ye see.
And 'twas 'ard if they'd be wasted like, and all along o' me.
And I'd lost me 'at and rifle—but I told you that before,
So I packed me mit inside me coat and "carried on" once more.
But the rumpus it was wicked, and the men were scarcer yet,
And I felt me ginger goin', but me jaws I kindo set,
And we passed the Boche first trenches, which was 'eapin' 'igh
with dead,
And we started for their second, which was fifty feet ahead;
When something like a 'ammer smashed me savage on the knee,
And down I came all muck and blood: Says I: "That's number
three."

So there I lay all 'elpless like, and bloody sick at that,
And worryin' like anythink, because I'd lost me 'at;
And thinkin' of me missis, and the partin' words she said:
"If you gets killed, write quick, ol' man, and tell me as you're
dead."
And lookin' at me bunch o' bombs—that was the 'ardest blow,
To think I'd never 'ave the chance to 'url them at the foe.
And there was all our boys in front, a-fightin' there like mad,
And me as could 'ave 'elped 'em wiv the lovely bombs I 'ad.
And so I cussed and cussed, and then I struggled back again,
Into that bit of battered trench, packed solid with its slain.

Now as I lay a-lyin' there and blastin' of me lot,
And wishin' I could just dispose of all them bombs I'd got,
I sees within the doorway of a shy, retirin' dug-out
Six Boches all a-grinnin', and their Captain stuck 'is mug out;
And they 'ad a nice machine gun, and I twigged what they was
at;
And they fixed it on a tripod, and I watched 'em like a cat;
And they got it in position, and they seemed so werry glad,
Like they'd got us in a death-trap, which, condemn their souls!
they 'ad.

For there our boys was fightin' fifty yards in front, and 'ere
This lousy bunch of Boches they 'ad got us in the rear.

Oh, it set me blood a-boilin' and I quite forgot me pain,
So I started crawlin', crawlin' over all them mounds of slain;
And them barstards was so busy-like they 'ad no eyes for me,
And me bleedin' leg was draggin', but me right arm it was
free. . . .
And now they 'ave it all in shape, and swingin' sweet and clear;
And now they're all excited like, but—I am drawin' near;
And now they 'ave it loaded up, and now they're takin'
aim. . . .
Rat-tat-tat-tat! Oh, here, says I, is where I join the game.
And my right arm it goes swingin', and a bomb it goes a-slingin',
And that "typewriter" goes wingin' in a thunderbolt of flame.

Then these Boches, wot was left of 'em, they tumbled down
their 'ole,
And up I climbed a mound of dead, and down on them I stole.
And, oh, that blessed moment when I heard their frightened yell,
And I laughed down in that dug-out, ere I bombed their souls
to hell.
And now I'm in the hospital, surprised that I'm alive;
We started out a thousand men, we came back thirty-five.
And I'm minus of a trotter, but I'm most amazin' gay,
For me bombs they wasn't wasted, though, you might say,
"thrown away."

The Atavist

What are you doing here, Tom Thorne, on the white top-knot o' the world,
Where the wind has the cut of a naked knife and the stars are rapier keen?
Hugging a smudgy willow fire, deep in a lynx robe curled,
You that's a lord's own son, Tom Thorne—what does your madness mean?

Go home, go home to your clubs, Tom Thorne! home to your evening dress!
Home to your place of power and pride, and the feast that waits for you!
Why do you linger all alone in the splendid emptiness,
Scouring the Land of the Little Sticks on the trail of the caribou?

Why did you fall off the Earth, Tom Thorne, out of our social ken?
What did your deep damnation prove? What was your dark despair?
Oh with the width of a world between, and years to the count of ten,
If they cut out your heart to-night, Tom Thorne, *Her* name would be graven there!

And you fled afar for the thing called Peace, and you thought you would find it here,
In the purple tundras vastly spread, and the mountains whitely piled;
It's a weary quest and a dreary quest, but I think that the end is near;
For they say that the Lord has hidden it in the secret heart of the Wild.

And you know that heart as few men know, and your eyes are
fey and deep,
With a "something lost" come welling back from the raw, red
dawn of life:
With woe and pain have you greatly lain, till out of abysmal
sleep
The soul of the Stone Age leaps in you, alert for the ancient
strife.

And if you came to our feast again, with its pomp and glee and
glow,
I think you would sit stone-still, Tom Thorne, and see in a daze
of dream,
A mad sun goading to frenzied flame the glittering gems of the
snow,
And a monster musk-ox bulking black against the blood-red
gleam.

I think you would see berg-battling shores, and stammer and halt
and stare,
With a sudden sense of the frozen void, serene and vast and still;
And the aching gleam and the hush of dream, and the track of
a great white bear,
And the primal lust that surged in you as you sprang to make
your kill.

I think you would hear the bull-moose call, and the glutted river
roar;
And spy the hosts of the caribou shadow the shining plain;
And feel the pulse of the Silences, and stand elate once more
On the verge of the yawning vastitudes that call to you in vain.

For I think you are one with the stars and the sun, and the wind
and the wave and the dew;
And the peaks untrod that yearn to God, and the valleys unde-
filed;
Men soar with wings, and they bridle kings, but what is it all to
you,
Wise in the ways of the wilderness, and strong with the strength
of the Wild?

You have spent your life, you have waged your strife where
never we play a part;
You have held the throne of the Great Unknown, you have
ruled a kingdom vast:

. . . .

*But to-night there's a strange, new trail for you, and you go, O
weary heart!*
*To the peace and rest of the Great Unguessed . . . at last, Tom
Thorne, at last.*

The Blind And The Dead

She lay like a saint on her copper couch;
    Like an angel asleep she lay,
In the stare of the ghoulish folks that slouch
    Past the Dead and sneak away.

Then came old Jules of the sightless gaze,
    Who begged in the streets for bread.
Each day he had come for a year of days,
    And groped his way to the Dead.

"What's the Devil's Harvest to-day?" he cried;
    "A wanton with eyes of blue!
I've known too many a such," he sighed;
    "Maybe I know this . . . mon Dieu!"

He raised the head of the heedless Dead;
He fingered the frozen face. . . .
Then a deathly spell on the watchers fell—
God! it was still, that place!

He raised the head of the careless Dead;
He fumbled a vagrant curl;
And then with his sightless smile he said:
"It's only my little girl."

"Dear, my dear, did they hurt you so!
Come to your daddy's heart. . . . "
Aye, and he held so tight, you know,
They were hard to force apart.

No! Paris isn't always gay;
And the morgue has its stories too:
You are a writer of tales, you say—
Then there is a tale for you.

The Ballad Of One-Eyed Mike

This is the tale that was told to me by the man with the crystal eye,
As I smoked my pipe in the camp-fire light, and the Glories swept the sky;
As the Northlights gleamed and curved and streamed, and the bottle of "hooch" was dry.

A man once aimed that my life be shamed, and wrought me a deathly wrong;
I vowed one day I would well repay, but the heft of his hate was strong.
He thonged me East and he thonged me West; he harried me back and forth,
Till I fled in fright from his peerless spite to the bleak, bald-headed North.

And there I lay, and for many a day I hatched plan after plan,
For a golden haul of the wherewithal to crush and to kill my man;
And there I strove, and there I clove through the drift of icy streams;
And there I fought, and there I sought for the pay-streak of my dreams.

So twenty years, with their hopes and fears and smiles and tears and such,
Went by and left me long bereft of hope of the Midas touch;
About as fat as a chancel rat, and lo! despite my will,
In the weary fight I had clean lost sight of the man I sought to kill.

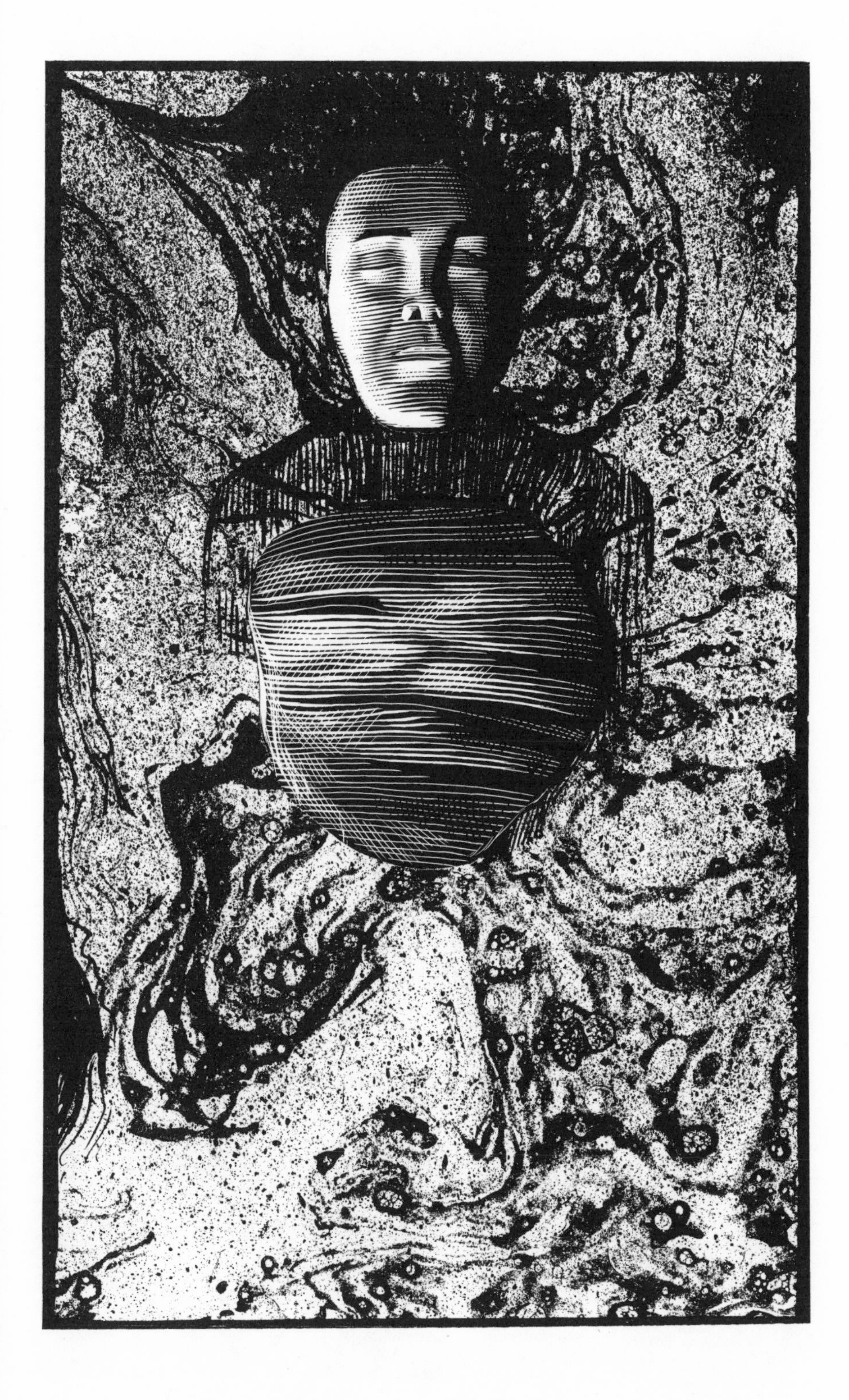

'Twas so far away, that evil day when I prayed the Prince of Gloom
For the savage strength and the sullen length of life to work his doom.
Nor sign nor word had I seen or heard, and it happed so long ago;
My youth was gone and my memory wan, and I willed it even so.

It fell one night in the waning light by the Yukon's oily flow,
I smoked and sat as I marvelled at the sky's port-winey glow;
Till it paled away to an absinthe gray, and the river seemed to shrink,
All wobbly flakes and wriggling snakes and goblin eyes a-wink.

'Twas weird to see and it 'wildered me in a queer, hypnotic dream,
Till I saw a spot like an inky blot come floating down the stream;
It bobbed and swung; it sheered and hung; it romped round in a ring;
It seemed to play in a tricksome way; it sure was a merry thing.

In freakish flights strange oily lights came fluttering round its head,
Like butterflies of a monster size—then I knew it for the Dead.
Its face was rubbed and slicked and scrubbed as smooth as a shaven pate;
In the silver snakes that the water makes it gleamed like a dinner-plate.

It gurgled near, and clear and clear and large and large it grew;
It stood upright in a ring of light and it looked me through and through.
It weltered round with a woozy sound, and ere I could retreat,
With the witless roll of a sodden soul it wantoned to my feet.

And here I swear by this Cross I wear, I heard that "floater" say:
"I am the man from whom you ran, the man you sought to slay.
That you may note and gaze and gloat and say 'Revenge is sweet,'
In the grit and grime of the river's slime I am rotting at your feet.

"The ill we rue we must e'en undo, though it rive us bone from bone;
So it came about that I sought you out, for I prayed I might atone.
I did you wrong, and for long and long I sought where you might live;
And now you're found, though I'm dead and drowned, I beg you to forgive."

So sad it seemed, and its cheek-bones gleamed, and its fingers flicked the shore;
And it lapped and lay in a weary way, and its hands met to implore;
That I gently said: "Poor, restless dead, I would never work you woe;
Though the wrong you rue you can ne'er undo, I forgave you long ago."

Then, wonder-wise, I rubbed my eyes and I woke from a horrid dream.
The moon rode high in the naked sky, and something bobbed in the stream.
It held my sight in a patch of light, and then it sheered from the shore;
It dipped and sank by a hollow bank, and I never saw it more.

This was the tale he told to me, that man so warped and gray,
Ere he slept and dreamed, and the camp-fire gleamed in his eye in a wolfish way—
That crystal eye that raked the sky in the weird Auroral ray.

The Man Who Knew

The Dreamer visioned Life as it might be,
And from his dream forthright a picture grew,
A painting all the people thronged to see,
And joyed therein—till came the Man Who Knew,
Saying: " 'Tis bad! Why do ye gape, ye fools!
He painteth not according to the schools."

The Dreamer probed Life's mystery of woe,
And in a book he sought to give the clue;
The people read, and saw that it was so,
And read again—then came the Man Who Knew
Saying: "Ye witless ones! this book is vile:
It hath not got the rudiments of style."

Love smote the Dreamer's lips, and silver clear
He sang a song so sweet, so tender true,
That all the market-place was thrilled to hear,
And listened rapt—till came the Man Who Knew,
Saying: "His technique's wrong; he singeth ill.
Waste not your time." The singer's voice was still.

And then the people roused as if from sleep,
Crying: "What care we if it be not Art!
Hath he not charmed us, made us laugh and weep?
Come, let us crown him where he sits apart."
Then, with his picture spurned, his book unread,
His song unsung, they found their Dreamer—*dead.*

The Song Of The Camp-Fire

I

Heed me, feed me, I am hungry, I am red-tongued with desire;
Boughs of balsam, slabs of cedar, gummy fagots of the pine,
Heap them on me, let me hug them to my eager heart of fire,
Roaring, soaring up to heaven as a symbol and a sign.
Bring me knots of sunny maple, silver birch and tamarack;
Leaping, sweeping, I will lap them with my ardent wings of flame;
I will kindle them to glory, I will beat the darkness back;
Streaming, gleaming, I will goad them to my glory and my fame.
Bring me gnarly limbs of live-oak, aid me in my frenzied fight;
Strips of iron-wood, scaly blue-gum, writhing redly in my hold;
With my lunge of lurid lances, with my whips that flail the night,
They will burgeon into beauty, they will foliate in gold.
Let me star the dim sierras, stab with light the inland seas;
Roaming wind and roaring darkness! seek no mercy at my hands;
I will mock the marly heavens, lamp the purple prairies,
I will flaunt my deathless banners down the far, unhouseled lands.
In the vast and vaulted pine-gloom where the pillared forests frown,
By the sullen, bestial rivers running where God only knows,
On the starlit coral beaches when the combers thunder down,
In the death-spell of the barrens, in the shudder of the snows;
In a blazing belt of triumph from the palm-leaf to the pine,
As a symbol of defiance lo! the wilderness I span;
And my beacons burn exultant as an everlasting sign
Of unending domination, of the mastery of Man;

I, the Life, the fierce Uplifter, I that weaned him from the mire;
I, the angel and the devil; I, the tyrant and the slave;
I, the Spirit of the Struggle; I, the mighty God of Fire·
I, the Maker and Destroyer; I, the Giver and the Grave.

II

Gather round me, boy and grey-beard, frontiersman of every kind.
Few are you, and far and lonely, yet an army forms behind:
By your camp-fires shall they know you, ashes scattered to the wind.

Peer into my heart of solace, break your bannock at my blaze;
Smoking, stretched in lazy shelter, build your castles as you gaze;
Or, it may be, deep in dreaming, think of dim, unhappy days.

Let my warmth and glow caress you, for your trails are grim and hard;
Let my arms of comfort press you, hunger-hewn and battle-scarred:
O my lovers! how I bless you with your lives so madly marred!

For you seek the silent spaces, and their secret lore you glean:
For you win the savage races, and the brutish Wild you wean;
And I gladden desert places, where camp-fire has never been.

From the Pole unto the Tropics is there trail ye have not dared?
And because you hold death lightly, so by death shall you be spared,
(As the sages of the ages in their pages have declared.)

On the roaring Arkilinik in a leaky bark canoe;
Up the cloud of Mount McKinley, where the avalanche leaps through;
In the furnace of Death Valley, when the mirage glimmers blue.

Now a smudge of wiry willows on the weary Kuskoquim;
Now a flare of gummy pine-knots where Vancouver's scaur is grim;
Now a gleam of sunny ceiba, when the Cuban beaches dim.

Always, always God's Great Open: lo! I burn with keener light
In the corridors of silence, in the vestibules of night;
'Mid the ferns and grasses gleaming, was there ever gem so bright?

Not for weaklings, not for women, like my brother of the hearth;
Ring your songs of wrath around me, I was made for manful mirth,
In the lusty, gusty greatness, on the bald spots of the earth.

Men, my masters! men, my lovers! ye have fought and ye have bled;
Gather round my ruddy embers, softly glowing is my bed;
By my heart of solace dreaming, rest ye and be comforted!

III

I am dying, O my masters! by my fitful flame ye sleep;
My purple plumes of glory droop forlorn.
Grey ashes choke and cloak me, and above the pines there creep
The stealthy silver moccasins of morn.
There comes a countless army, it's the Legion of the Light;
It tramps in gleaming triumph round the world;
And before its jewelled lances all the shadows of the night
Back in to abysmal darknesses are hurled.

Leap to life again, my lovers! ye must toil and never tire;
The day of daring, doing, brightens clear,
When the bed of spicy cedar and the jovial camp-fire
Must only be a memory of cheer.
There is hope and golden promise in the vast portentous dawn;
There is glamour in the glad, effluent sky:
Go and leave me; I will dream of you and love you when you're gone;
I have served you, O my masters! let me die.

A little heap of ashes, grey and sodden by the rain,
Wind-scattered, blurred and blotted by the snow:
Let that be all to tell of me, and glorious again,
Ye things of greening gladness, leap and glow!

A black scar in the sunshine by the palm-leaf or the pine,
    Blind to the night and dead to all desire;
Yet oh, of life and uplift what a symbol and a sign!
Yet oh, of power and conquest what a destiny is mine!
A little heap of ashes— Yea! a miracle divine,
    The foot-print of a god, all-radiant Fire.

The Low-Down White

This is the pay-day up at the mines, when the bearded brutes
come down;
There's money to burn in the streets to-night so I've sent my
klooch to town,
With a haggard face and a ribband of red entwined in her hair
of brown.

And I know at the dawn she'll come reeling home with the
bottles, one, two, three—
One for herself, to drown her shame, and two big bottles for me,
To make me forget the thing I am and the man I used to be.

To make me forget the brand of the dog, as I crouch in this
hideous place;
To make me forget once I kindled the light of love in a lady's
face,
Where even the squalid Siwash now holds me a black disgrace.

Oh, I have guarded my secret well! And who would dream as I
speak
In a tribal tongue like a rogue unhung, 'mid the ranch-house
filth and reek,
I could roll to bed with a Latin phrase and rise with a verse of
Greek?

Yet I was a senior prizeman once, and the pride of a college
eight;
Called to the bar—my friends were true! but they could not
keep me straight;
Then came the divorce, and I went abroad and "died" on the
River Plate.

But I'm not dead yet; though with half a lung there isn't time
to spare,
And I hope that the year will see me out, and, thank God, no one
will care—
Save maybe the little slim Siwash girl with the rose of shame in
her hair.

She will come with the dawn, and the dawn is near; I can see its
evil glow,
Like a corpse-light seen through a frosty pane in a night of want
and woe;
And yonder she comes by the bleak bull-pines, swift staggering
through the snow.

The Hat

In city shop a hat I saw
That so my fancy seemed to strike,
I gave my wage to buy the straw,
And make myself a one the like.

I wore it to the village fair;
Oh proud I was, though poor was I.
The maids looked at me with a stare,
The lads looked at me with a sigh.

I wore it Sunday to the Mass.
The other girls wore handkerchiefs.
I saw them darkly watch and pass,
With sullen smiles, the hidden griefs.

And then with sobbing fear I fled,
But they waylayed me on the street,
And tore the hat from off my head,
And trampled it beneath their feet.

I sought the Church; my grief was wild,
And by my mother's grave I sat:
. . . I've never cried for clay-cold child,
As I wept for that ruined hat.

The Haggis Of Private McPhee

"Hae ye heard whit ma auld mither's postit tae me?
It fair maks me hamesick," says Private McPhee.
"And whit did she send ye?" says Private McPhun,
As he cockit his rifle and bleezed at a Hun.
"A haggis! A *Haggis!*" says Private McPhee;
"The brawest big haggis I ever did see.
And think! it's the morn when fond memory turns
Tae haggis and whuskey—the Birthday o' Burns.
We maun find a dram; then we'll ca' in the rest
O' the lads, and we'll hae a Burns' Nicht wi' the best."

"Be ready at sundoon," snapped Sergeant McCole;
"I want you two men for the List'nin' Patrol."
Then Private McPhee looked at Private McPhun:
"I'm thinkin', ma lad, we're confoundedly done."
Then Private McPhun looked at Private McPhee:
"I'm thinkin' auld chap, it's a' aff wi' oor spree."
But up spoke their crony, wee Wullie McNair:
"Jist lea' yer braw haggis for me tae prepare;
And as for the dram, if I search the camp roun',
We maun hae a drappie tae jist haud it doon.
Sae rin, lads, and think, though the nicht it be black,
O' the haggis that's waitin' ye when ye get back."

My! but it wis waesome on Naebuddy's Land,
And the deid they were rottin' on every hand.
And the rockets like corpse candles hauntit the sky,
And the winds o' destruction went shudderin' by.
There wis skelpin' o' bullets and skirlin' o' shells,

And breengin' o' bombs and a thoosand death-knells;
But cooryin' doon in a Jack Johnson hole
Little fashed the twa men o' the List'nin' Patrol.
For sweeter than honey and bricht as a gem
Wis the thocht o' the haggis that waitit for them.

Yet alas! in oor moments o' sunniest cheer
Calamity's aften maist cruelly near.
And while the twa talked o' their puddin' divine
The Boches below them were howkin' a mine.
And while the twa cracked o' the feast they would hae,
The fuse it wis burnin' and burnin' away.
Then sudden a roar like the thunner o' doom,
A hell-leap o' flame . . . then the wheesht o' the tomb.

"Haw, Jock! Are ye hurtit?" says Private McPhun.
"Ay, Geordie, they've got me; I'm fearin' I'm done.
It's ma leg; I'm jist thinkin' it's aff at the knee;
Ye'd best gang and leave me," says Private McPhee.
"Oh leave ye I wunna," says Private McPhun;
"And leave ye I canna, for though I micht run,
It's no faur I wud gang, it's no muckle I'd see:
I'm blindit, and that's whit's the maitter wi' me."
Then Private McPhee sadly shakit his heid:
"If we bide here for lang, we'll be bidin' for deid.
And yet, Geordie lad, I could gang weel content
If I'd tasted that haggis ma auld mither sent."
"That's droll," says McPhun; "ye've jist speakit ma mind.
Oh I ken it's a terrible thing tae be blind;
And yet it's no that that embitters ma lot—
It's missin' that braw muckle haggis ye've got."
For a while they were silent; then up once again
Spoke Private McPhee, though he whussilt wi' pain:
"And why should we miss it? Between you and me
We've legs for tae run, and we've eyes for tae see.
You lend me your shanks and I'll lend you ma sicht,
And we'll baith hae a kyte-fu' o' haggis the nicht."

Oh the sky it wis dourlike and dreepin' a wee,
When Private McPhun gruppit Private McPhee.
Oh the glaur it wis fylin' and crieshin' the grun',

When Private McPhee guidit Private McPhun.
"Keep clear o' them corpses—they're maybe no deid!
Haud on! There's a big muckle crater aheid.
Look oot! There's a sap; we'll be haein' a coup.
A staur-shell! For Godsake! Doun, lad, on yer daup.
Bear aff tae yer richt. . . . Aw yer jist daein' fine:
Before the nicht's feenished on haggis we'll dine."

There wis death and destruction on every hand;
There wis havoc and horror on Naebuddy's Land.
And the shells bickered doun wi' a crump and a glare,
And the hameless wee bullets were dingin' the air,
Yet on they went staggerin', cooryin' doun
When the stutter and cluck o' a Maxim crept roun'.
And the legs o' McPhun they were sturdy and stoot,
And McPhee on his back kept a bonnie look-oot.
"On, on, ma brave lad! We're no faur frae the goal;
I can hear the braw sweerin' o' Sergeant McCole."

But strength has its leemit, and Private McPhun,
Wi' a sab and a curse fell his length on the grun'.
Then Private McPhee shoutit doon in his ear:
"Jist think o' the haggis! I smell it from here.
It's gushin' wi' juice, it's embaumin' the air;
It's steamin' for us, and we're—jist—aboot—there."
Then Private McPhun answers: "Dommit, auld chap!
For the sake o' that haggis I'll gang till I drap."
And he gets on his feet wi' a heave and a strain,
And onward he staggers in passion and pain.
And the flare and the glare and the fury increase,
Till you'd think they'd jist taken a' hell on a lease.
And on they go reelin' in peetifu' plight,
And someone is shoutin' away on their right;
And someone is runnin', and noo they can hear
A sound like a prayer and a sound like a cheer;
And swift through the crash and the flash and the din,
The lads o' the Hielands are bringin' them in.

"They're baith sairly woundit, but is it no droll
Hoo they rave aboot haggis?" says Sergeant McCole.
When hirplin alang comes wee Wullie McNair,

And they a' wonnert why he wis greetin' sae sair.
And he says: "I'd jist liftit it oot o' the pot,
And there it lay steamin' and savoury hot,
When sudden I dooked at the fleech o' a shell,
And it—*drapped on the haggis and dinged it tae hell.*"

And oh but the lads were fair taken aback;
Then sudden the order wis passed tae attack,
And up from the trenches like lions they leapt,
And on through the nicht like a torrent they swept.
On, on, wi' their bayonets thirstin' before!
On, on tae the foe wi' a rush and a roar!
And wild to the welkin their battle-cry rang,
And doon on the Boches like tigers they sprang:
And there wisna a man but had death in his ee,
For he thocht o' the haggis o' Private McPhee.

The Call Of The Wild

Have you gazed on naked grandeur where there's nothing else
to gaze on,
Set pieces and drop-curtain scenes galore,
Big mountains heaved to heaven, which the blinding sunsets
blazon,
Black canyons where the rapids rip and roar?
Have you swept the visioned valley with the green stream streak-
ing through it,
Searched the Vastness for a something you have lost?
Have you strung your soul to silence? Then for God's sake go
and do it;
Hear the challenge, learn the lesson, pay the cost.

Have you wandered in the wilderness, the sagebrush desolation,
The bunch-grass levels where the cattle graze?

Have you whistled bits of rag-time at the end of all creation,
And learned to know the desert's little ways?
Have you camped upon the foothills, have you galloped o'er the ranges,
Have you roamed the arid sun-lands through and through?
Have you chummed up with the mesa? Do you know its moods and changes?
Then listen to the Wild—it's calling you.

Have you known the Great White Silence, not a snow-gemmed twig aquiver?
(Eternal truths that shame our soothing lies.)
Have you broken trail on snowshoes? mushed your huskies up the river,
Dared the unknown, led the way, and clutched the prize?
Have you marked the map's void spaces, mingled with the mongrel races,
Felt the savage strength of brute in every thew?
And though grim as hell the worst is, can you round it off with curses?
Then hearken to the Wild—it's wanting you.

Have you suffered, starved and triumphed, groveled down, yet grasped at glory,
Grown bigger in the bigness of the whole?
"Done things" just for the doing, letting babblers tell the story,
Seeing through the nice veneer the naked soul?
Have you seen God in His splendors, heard the text that nature renders?
(You'll never hear it in the family pew.)
The simple things, the true things, the silent men who do things—
Then listen to the Wild—it's calling you.

They have cradled you in custom, they have primed you with their preaching,
They have soaked you in convention through and through;
They have put you in a showcase; you're a credit to their teaching—
But can't you hear the Wild?—it's calling you.

Let us probe the silent places, let us seek what luck betide us;
  Let us journey to a lonely land I know.
There's a whisper on the night-wind, there's a star agleam to
    guide us,
  And the Wild is calling, calling . . . let us go.

The Lone Trail

Ye who know the Lone Trail fain would follow it,
Though it lead to glory or the darkness of the pit.
Ye who take the Lone Trail, bid your love good-by;
The Lone Trail, the Lone Trail follow till you die.

The trails of the world be countless, and most of the trails be tried;
You tread on the heels of the many, till you come where the ways divide;
And one lies safe in the sunlight, and the other is dreary and wan,
Yet you look aslant at the Lone Trail, and the Lone Trail lures you on.
And somehow you're sick of the highway, with its noise and its easy needs,
And you seek the risk of the by-way, and you reck not where it leads.
And sometimes it leads to the desert, and the tongue swells out of the mouth,
And you stagger blind to the mirage, to die in the mocking drouth.
And sometimes it leads to the mountain, to the light of the lone camp-fire,
And you gnaw your belt in the anguish of hunger-goaded desire.
And sometimes it leads to the Southland, to the swamp where the orchid glows,
And you rave to your grave with the fever, and they rob the corpse for its clothes.
And sometimes it leads to the Northland, and the scurvy softens your bones,
And your flesh dints in like putty, and you spit out your teeth like stones.

And sometimes it leads to a coral reef in the wash of a weedy sea,
And you sit and stare at the empty glare where the gulls wait greedily.
And sometimes it leads to an Arctic trail, and the snows where your torn feet freeze,
And you whittle away the useless clay, and crawl on your hands and knees.
Often it leads to the dead-pit; always it leads to pain;
By the bones of your brothers ye know it, but oh, to follow you're fain.
By your bones they will follow behind you, till the ways of the world are made plain.

Bid good-by to sweetheart, bid good-by to friend;
The Lone Trail, the Lone Trail follow to the end.
Tarry not, and fear not, chosen of the true;
Lover of the Lone Trail, the Lone Trail waits for you.

Lost

"Black is the sky, but the land is white—
(O the wind, the snow and the storm!)—
Father, where is our boy to-night?
Pray to God he is safe and warm."

"Mother, mother, why should you fear?
Safe is he, and the Arctic moon
Over his cabin shines so clear—
Rest and sleep, 'twill be morning soon."

"It's getting dark awful sudden. Say, this is mighty queer!
Where in the world have I got to? It's still and black as a tomb.
I reckoned the camp was yonder, I figured the trail was here—
Nothing! Just draw and valley packed with quiet and gloom:
Snow that comes down like feathers, thick and gobby and gray;
Night that looks spiteful ugly—seems that I've lost my way.

"The cold's got an edge like a jackknife—it must be forty below;
Leastways that's what it seems like—it cuts so fierce to the bone.
The wind's getting real ferocious; it's heaving and whirling the snow;
It shrieks with a howl of fury, it dies away to a moan;
Its arms sweep round like a banshee's, swift and icily white,
And buffet and blind and beat me. Lord! it's a hell of a night.

"I'm all tangled up in a blizzard. There's only one thing to do—
Keep on moving and moving; it's death, it's death if I rest.
Oh, God! if I see the morning, if only I struggle through,
I'll say the prayers I've forgotten since I lay on my mother's breast.

I seem going round in a circle; maybe the camp is near.
Say! did somebody holler? Was it a light I saw?
Or was it only a notion? I'll shout, and maybe they'll hear—
No! the wind only drowns me—shout till my throat is raw.

"The boys are all round the camp-fire wondering when I'll be back.
They'll soon be starting to seek me; they'll scarcely wait for the light.
What will they find, I wonder, when they come to the end of my track—
A hand stuck out of a snowdrift, frozen and stiff and white.
That's what they'll strike, I reckon; that's how they'll find their pard,
A pie-faced corpse in a snowbank—curse you, don't be a fool!
Play the game to the finish; bet on your very last card;
Nerve yourself for the struggle. Oh, you coward, keep cool!

"I'm going to lick this blizzard; I'm going to live the night.
It can't down me with its bluster—I'm not the kind to be beat.
On hands and knees will I buck it; with every breath will I fight;
It's life, it's life that I fight for—never it seemed so sweet.
I know that my face is frozen; my hands are numblike and dead;
But oh, my feet keep a-moving, heavy and hard and slow;
They're trying to kill me, kill me, the night that's black over-head,
The wind that cuts like a razor, the whipcord lash of the snow.
Keep a-moving, a-moving; don't, don't stumble, you fool!
Curse this snow that's a-piling a-purpose to block my way.
It's heavy as gold in the rocker, it's white and fleecy as wool;
It's soft as a bed of feathers, it's warm as a stack of hay.
Curse on my feet that slip so, my poor tired, stumbling feet—
I guess they're a job for the surgeon, they feel so queerlike to lift—
I'll rest them just for a moment—oh, but to rest is sweet!
The awful wind cannot get me, deep, deep down in the drift."

"Father, a bitter cry I heard,
Out of the night so dark and wild.

Why is my heart so strangely stirred?
'Twas like the voice of our erring child."

"Mother, mother, you only heard
A waterfowl in the locked lagoon—
Out of the night a wounded bird—
Rest and sleep, 'twill be morning soon."

Who is it talks of sleeping? I'll swear that somebody shook
Me hard by the arm for a moment, but how on earth could it be?
See how my feet are moving—awfully funny they look—
Moving as if they belonged to a someone that wasn't me.
The wind down the night's long alley bowls me down like a pin;
I stagger and fall and stagger, crawl arm-deep in the snow.
Beaten back to my corner, how can I hope to win?
And there is the blizzard waiting to give me the knockout blow.

Oh, I'm so warm and sleepy! No more hunger and pain.
Just to rest for a moment; was ever rest such a joy?
Ha! what was that? I'll swear it, somebody shook me again;
Somebody seemed to whisper: "Fight to the last, my boy."
Fight! That's right, I must struggle. I know that to rest means death;
Death, but then what does death mean?—ease from a world of strife.
Life has been none too pleasant; yet with my failing breath
Still and still must I struggle, fight for the gift of life.

. . . .

Seems that I must be dreaming! Here is the old home trail;
Yonder a light is gleaming; oh, I know it so well!
The air is scented with clover; the cattle wait by the rail;
Father is through with the milking; there goes the supper-bell.

. . . .

Mother, your boy is crying, out in the night and cold;
Let me in and forgive me, I'll never be bad any more:
I'm, oh, so sick and so sorry: please, dear mother, don't scold—
It's just your boy, and he wants you. . . . Mother, open the door. . . .

LOST

"Father, father, I saw a face
Pressed just now to the window-pane!
Oh, it gazed for a moment's space,
Wild and wan, and was gone again!"

"Mother, mother, you saw the snow
Drifted down from the maple tree
(Oh, the wind that is sobbing so!
Weary and worn and old are we)—
Only the snow and a wounded loon—
Rest and sleep, 'twill be morning soon."

The Lure Of Little Voices

There's a cry from out the loneliness—oh, listen, Honey, listen!
Do you hear it, do you fear it, you're a-holding of me so?
You're a-sobbing in your sleep, dear, and your lashes, how they glisten—
Do you hear the Little Voices all a-begging me to go?

All a-begging me to leave you. Day and night they're pleading, praying,
On the North-wind, on the West-wind, from the peak and from the plain;
Night and day they never leave me—do you know what they are saying?
"He was ours before you got him, and we want him once again."

Yes, they're wanting me, they're haunting me, the awful lonely places;
They're whining and they're whimpering as if each had a soul;
They're calling from the wilderness, the vast and God-like spaces,
The stark and sullen solitudes that sentinel the Pole.

They miss my little camp-fires, ever brightly, bravely gleaming
In the womb of desolation, where was never man before;
As comradeless I sought them, lion-hearted, loving, dreaming,
And they hailed me as a comrade, and they loved me evermore.

And now they're all a-crying, and it's no use me denying;
The spell of them is on me and I'm helpless as a child;
My heart is aching, aching, but I hear them, sleeping, waking;
It's the Lure of Little Voices, it's the mandate of the Wild.

I'm afraid to tell you, Honey, I can take no bitter leaving;
But softly in the sleep-time from your love I'll steal away.
Oh, it's cruel, dearie, cruel, and it's God knows how I'm grieving;
But His loneliness is calling, and He knows I must obey.

The March Of The Dead

The cruel war was over—oh, the triumph was so sweet!
  We watched the troops returning, through our tears;
There was triumph, triumph, triumph down the scarlet glittering street,
  And you scarce could hear the music for the cheers.
And you scarce could see the house-tops for the flags that flew between;
  The bells were pealing madly to the sky;
And everyone was shouting for the Soldiers of the Queen,
  And the glory of an age was passing by.

And then there came a shadow, swift and sudden, dark and drear;
  The bells were silent, not an echo stirred.
The flags were drooping sullenly, the men forgot to cheer;
  We waited, and we never spoke a word.
The sky grew darker, darker, till from out the gloomy rack
  There came a voice that checked the heart with dread:
"Tear down, tear down your bunting now, and hang up sable black;
  They are coming—it's the Army of the Dead."

They were coming, they were coming, gaunt and ghastly, sad and slow;
  They were coming, all the crimson wrecks of pride;
With faces seared, and cheeks red smeared, and haunting eyes of woe,
  And clotted holes the khaki couldn't hide.

Oh, the clammy brow of anguish! the livid, foam-flecked lips!
  The reeling ranks of ruin swept along!
The limb that trailed, the hand that failed, the bloody finger tips!
  And oh, the dreary rhythm of their song!

"They left us on the veldt-side, but we felt we couldn't stop
  On this, our England's crowning festal day;
We're the men of Magersfontein, we're the men of Spion Kop,
  Colenso—we're the men who had to pay.
We're the men who paid the blood-price. Shall the grave be all
    our gain?
  You owe us. Long and heavy is the score.
Then cheer us for our glory now, and cheer us for our pain,
  And cheer us as ye never cheered before."

The folks were white and stricken, and each tongue seemed
    weighted with lead;
  Each heart was clutched in hollow hand of ice;
And every eye was staring at the horror of the dead,
  The pity of the men who paid the price.
They were come, were come to mock us, in the first flush of our
    peace;
  Through writhing lips their teeth were all agleam;
They were coming in their thousands—oh, would they never
    cease!
  I closed my eyes, and then—it was a dream.

There was triumph, triumph, triumph down the scarlet gleam-
    ing street;
  The town was mad; a man was like a boy.
A thousand flags were flaming where the sky and city meet;
  A thousand bells were thundering the joy.
There was music, mirth and sunshine; but some eyes shone with
    regret;
  And while we stun with cheers our homing braves,
O God, in Thy great mercy, let us nevermore forget
  The graves they left behind, the bitter graves.

The Song Of The Pacifist

What do they matter, our headlong hates, when we take the toll of our Dead?
Think ye our glory and gain will pay for the torrent of blood we have shed?
By the cheers of our Victory will the heart of the mother be comforted?

If by the Victory all we mean is a broken and brooding foe;
Is the pomp and power of a glitt'ring hour, and a truce for an age or so:
By the clay-cold hand on the broken blade we have smitten a bootless blow!

If by the Triumph we only prove that the sword we sheathe is bright;
That justice and truth and love endure; that freedom's throned on the height;
That the feebler folks shall be unafraid; that Might shall never be Right;

If this be all: by the blood-drenched plains, by the havoc of fire and fear,
By the rending roar of the War of Wars, by the Dead so doubly dear. . . .
Then our Victory is a vast defeat, and it mocks us as we cheer.

Victory! there can be but one, hallowed in every land:
When by the graves of our common dead we who were foemen stand;
And in the hush of our common grief hand is tendered to hand.

Triumph! Yes, when out of the dust in the splendour of their release
The spirits of those who fell go forth and they hallow our hearts to peace,
And, brothers in pain, with world-wide voice, we clamour that War shall cease.

Glory! Ay, when from blackest loss shall be born most radiant gain;
When over the gory fields shall rise a star that never shall wane:
Then, and then only, our Dead shall know that they have not fall'n in vain.

When our children's children shall talk of War as a madness that may not be;
When we thank our God for our grief to-day, and blazon from sea to sea
In the name of the Dead the banner of Peace . . . *that will be Victory*.

The Law Of The Yukon

This is the law of the Yukon, and ever she makes it plain:
"Send not your foolish and feeble; send me your strong and your sane—
Strong for the red rage of battle; sane, for I harry them sore;
Send me men girt for the combat, men who are grit to the core;
Swift as the panther in triumph, fierce as the bear in defeat,
Sired of a bulldog parent, steeled in the furnace heat.
Send me the best of your breeding, lend me your chosen ones;
Them will I take to my bosom, them will I call my sons;
Them will I gild with my treasure, them will I glut with my meat;
But the others—the misfits, the failures—I trample under my feet.
Dissolute, damned and despairful, crippled and palsied and slain,
Ye would send me the spawn of your gutters— Go! take back your spawn again.

"Wild and wide are my borders, stern as death is my sway;
From my ruthless throne I have ruled alone for a million years and a day;
Hugging my mighty treasure, waiting for man to come,
Till he swept like a turbid torrent, and after him swept—the scum.
The pallid pimp of the dead-line, the enervate of the pen,
One by one I weeded them out, for all that I sought was—Men.
One by one I dismayed them, frighting them sore with my glooms;

One by one I betrayed them unto my manifold dooms.
Drowned them like rats in my rivers, starved them like curs on
my plains,
Rotted the flesh that was left them, poisoned the blood in their
veins;
Burst with my winter upon them, searing forever their sight,
Lashed them with fungus-white faces, whimpering wild in the
night;

"Staggering blind through the storm-whirl, stumbling mad
through the snow,
Frozen stiff in the ice-pack, brittle and bent like a bow;
Featureless, formless, forsaken, scented by wolves in their
flight,
Left for the wind to make music through ribs that are glitter-
ing white;
Gnawing the black crust of failure, searching the pit of despair,
Crooking the toe in the trigger, trying to patter a prayer;
Going outside with an escort, raving with lips all afoam,
Writing a cheque for a million, driveling feebly of home;
Lost like a louse in the burning . . . or else in the tented town
Seeking a drunkard's solace, sinking and sinking down;
Steeped in the slime at the bottom, dead to a decent world,
Lost 'mid the human flotsam, far on the frontier hurled;
In the camp at the bend of the river, with its dozen saloons
aglare,
Its gambling dens ariot, its gramophones all ablare;
Crimped with the crimes of a city, sin-ridden and bridled with
lies,
In the hush of my mountained vastness, in the flush of my mid-
night skies.
Plague-spots, yet tools of my purpose, so natheless I suffer
them thrive,
Crushing my Weak in their clutches, that only my Strong may
survive.

"But the others, the men of my mettle, the men who would
'stablish my fame
Unto its ultimate issue, winning me honor, not shame;
Searching my uttermost valleys, fighting each step as they go,

Shooting the wrath of my rapids, scaling my ramparts of snow;
Ripping the guts of my mountains, looting the beds of my creeks,
Them will I take to my bosom, and speak as a mother speaks.
I am the land that listens, I am the land that broods;
Steeped in eternal beauty, crystalline waters and woods.
Long have I waited lonely, shunned as a thing accurst,
Monstrous, moody, pathetic, the last of the lands and the first;
Visioning camp-fires at twilight, sad with a longing forlorn,
Feeling my womb o'er-pregnant with the seed of cities unborn.
Wild and wide are my borders, stern as death is my sway,
And I wait for the men who will win me—and I will not be won in a day;
And I will not be won by weaklings, subtle, suave and mild,
But by men with the hearts of vikings, and the simple faith of a child;
Desperate, strong and resistless, unthrottled by fear or defeat,
Them will I gild with my treasure, them will I glut with my meat.

"Lofty I stand from each sister land, patient and wearily wise,
With the weight of a world of sadness in my quiet, passionless eyes;

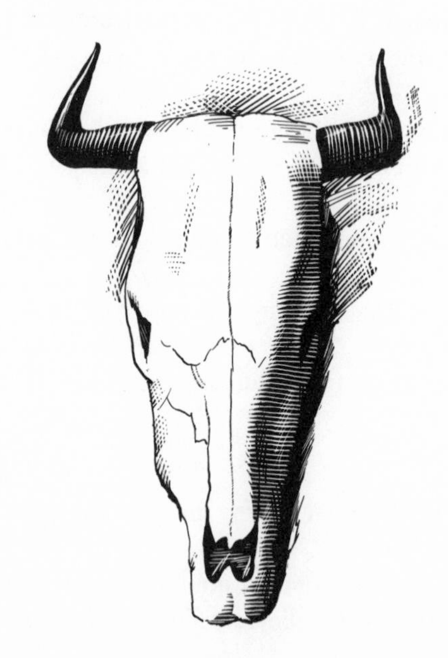

Dreaming alone of a people, dreaming alone of a day,
When men shall not rape my riches, and curse me and go away;
Making a bawd of my bounty, fouling the hand that gave—
Till I rise in my wrath and I sweep on their path and I stamp
them into a grave.
Dreaming of men who will bless me, of women esteeming me
good,
Of children born in my borders of radiant motherhood,
Of cities leaping to stature, of fame like a flag unfurled,
As I pour the tide of my riches in the eager lap of the world."

This is the Law of the Yukon, that only the Strong shall thrive;
That surely the Weak shall perish, and only the Fit survive.
Dissolute, damned and despairful, crippled and palsied and slain,
This is the Will of the Yukon,— Lo, how she makes it plain!

The Logger

In the moonless, misty night, with my little pipe alight,
I am sitting by the camp-fire's fading cheer;
Oh, the dew is falling chill on the dim, deer-haunted hill,
And the breakers in the bay are moaning drear.
The toilful hours are sped, the boys are long abed,
And I alone a weary vigil keep;
In the sightless, sullen sky I can hear the night-hawk cry,
And the frogs in frenzied chorus from the creek.

And somehow the embers' glow brings me back the long ago,
The days of merry laughter and light song;
When I sped the hours away with the gayest of the gay
In the giddy whirl of fashion's festal throng.
Oh, I ran a grilling race and I little recked the pace,
For the lust of youth ran riot in my blood;
But at last I made a stand in this God-forsaken land
Of the pine-tree and the mountain and the flood.

And now I've got to stay, with an overdraft to pay,
For pleasure in the past with future pain;
And I'm not the chap to whine, for if the chance were mine
I know I'd choose the old life once again.
With its woman's eyes a-shine, and its flood of golden wine,
Its fever and its frolic and its fun;
The old life with its din, its laughter and its sin—
And chuck me in the gutter when it's done.

Ah, well! it's past and gone, and the memory is wan,
That conjures up each old familiar face;
And here by fortune hurled, I am dead to all the world,
And I've learned to lose my pride and keep my place.

THE LOGGER

My ways are hard and rough, and my arms are strong and tough,
And I hew the dizzy pine till darkness falls;
And sometimes I take a dive, just to keep my heart alive,
Among the gay saloons and dancing halls.

In the distant, dinful town just a little drink to drown
The cares that crowd and canker in my brain;
Just a little joy to still set my pulses all a-thrill,
Then back to brutish labour once again.
And things will go on so until one day I shall know
That Death has got me cinched beyond a doubt;
Then I'll crawl away from sight, and morosely in the night
My weary, wasted life will peter out.

Then the boys will gather round, and they'll launch me in the ground,
And pile the stones the timber wolf to foil;
And the moaning pine will wave overhead a nameless grave,
Where the black snake in the sunshine loves to coil.
And they'll leave me there alone, and perhaps with softened tone
Speak of me sometimes in the camp-fire's glow,
As a played-out, broken chum, who has gone to Kingdom Come,
And who went the pace in England long ago.

Good-Bye, Little Cabin

O dear little cabin, I've loved you so long,
And now I must bid you good-bye!
I've filled you with laughter, I've thrilled you with song
And sometimes I've wished I could cry.
Your walls they have witnessed a weariful fight,
And rung to a won Waterloo:
But oh, in my triumph I'm dreary to-night—
Good-bye, little cabin, to you!

Your roof is bewhiskered, your floor is a-slant,
Your walls seem to sag and to swing;
I'm trying to find just your faults, but I can't—
You poor, tired, heart-broken old thing!
I've seen when you've been the best friend that I had
Your light like a gem on the snow;
You're sort of a part of me— Gee! but I'm sad;
I hate, little cabin, to go.

Below your cracked window red raspberries climb;
A hornet's nest hangs from a beam;
Your rafters are scribbled with adage and rhyme,
And dimmed with tobacco and dream.
"Each day has its laugh," and "Don't worry, just work."
Such mottoes reproachfully shine.
Old calendars dangle—what memories lurk
About you, dear cabin of mine!

I hear the world-call and the clang of the fight;
I hear the hoarse cry of my kind;

Yet well do I know, as I quit you to-night,
It's Youth that I'm leaving behind.
And often I'll think of you, empty and black,
Moose antlers nailed over your door:
Oh, if I should perish my ghost will come back
To dwell in you, cabin, once more!

How cold, still and lonely, how weary you seem!
A last wistful look and I'll go.
Oh, will you remember the lad with his dream!
The lad that you comforted so.
The shadows enfold you, it's drawing to-night;
The evening star needles the sky:
And huh! but it's stinging and stabbing my sight—
God bless you, old cabin, good-bye!

Index Of First Lines